beautiful baking

Jane Asher

beautiful
baking

SIMON &
SCHUSTER

London New York Sydney Toronto

First published in Great Britain by Simon & Schuster UK Ltd 2007
A CBS Company

This edition printed 2009 for Index Books Ltd

Copyright © Jane Asher

Simon & Schuster UK Ltd
222 Grays Inn Road
London WC1X 8HB

3 5 7 9 10 8 6 4 2

Design: Gabriella Le Grazie
Photography: Sam Bailey
Prop styling: Sarah Walker
Cover design: Raffaela Romaya

Printed and bound in China
ISBN   978-1-84737-044-0 hardback

Acknowledgements

With huge thanks for their encouragement and support to: Janet Copleston, Emma Marks, Sam Bailey, Sarah Walker, Ruth Clark, David Trumper, Gabriella Le Grazie, Stuart Polson and Angie Bojanowski.

And, as always, my gratitude to my lovely, greedy family, whose enthusiastic, if sometimes critical, appreciation of my cooking makes them such a joy to feed.

Dedication
For Gordon and Joyce, with love

contents

INTRODUCTION

The cake books that I've written over the years have all been concerned with the highly decorated celebration cakes that are brought out for birthdays, weddings and so on, but – as you can imagine – at home in the Scarfe household we don't tuck into tiered, iced reproductions of the Albert Memorial every weekend, and the baking that I do in my own kitchen for my family is what this book is all about.

I learnt all my basic cooking skills – and my love of food – during my childhood and early teens; firstly from watching my Mum, and 'helping' her make fairy cakes, well-fingered gingerbread men and so on and, later, from evening classes given by my local council in general cookery (at 7/6d a term – that's 35p to you). Family life inevitably having changed in many ways since then, there are fewer opportunities for many of us to experience home cooking, and home baking in particular has dwindled in popularity over the years (although recently it seemed to have been undergoing a renaissance, thanks to wonderful TV cooks such as Nigella and Jamie).

I worked on this book at weekends, which tends to be the time I do most of my baking in any case, and I tested every single recipe – and many more that I discounted – at home in my kitchen as I wrote it out (and re-baked many of them several times, to make sure I had the best possible version and one that would be as foolproof as possible), and then baked them all again for the photographs. No home economists, recipe testers, professional chefs, digital enhancement, or anything else that you wouldn't have at home, have been involved, so you should be able to make everything in the book in exactly the same way. I enjoyed all of it (except perhaps the mounds of washing up that testing and re-testing 60 or so cakes created – so I did ask a friend to help me clear up, or we'd never have got them all done in the six days allocated and I would have been a nervous wreck).

These are not all classic cakes, by any means: it's a mixture of some of my old favourites, variations on popular traditional treats and a few brand-new ideas. There are plenty I adore that I haven't been able to include, but I hope you'll be inspired to try many more cake recipes once you've made some of these.

The amount of pleasure that putting a home-baked cake on the table produces – both for the cook and for those eating it – is out of all proportion to the work involved. There really is very little mystique or complicated skill to making a cake, biscuit or loaf of bread, and yet the sense of smug satisfaction you get as you place it carefully on a plate and stand back to bask in glory, is enormous. It's partly, of course, because a cake is far more than just a piece of food: it's a symbol, a centrepiece and a reassuring token of (oh dear, can I really get this pretentious?) love. Well it is – so there. Even a simple question like: 'why don't you come in and have a cup of tea and a slice of cake?' has something cosy, comforting and caring about it (now she's not only pretentious, but alliterative as well.. just shut up Jane, and get on with the recipes...)

EQUIPMENT

I haven't used anything particularly fancy in any of the recipes, but there are a few pieces of equipment well worth having.

ELECTRIC MIXER

I've assumed that you have access to some kind of electric mixer, but if you want to work with a copper bowl and hand whisk then, of course, that's your prerogative – you're far less lazy and impatient than I am. It is much easier, though, to get good results for cakes and icings if you do have a mixer, so if you don't, I'd seriously consider investing in one or putting it on a birthday list. Either a hand-held or a free-standing one is going to be useful, but if you have both… then life gets really simple. I have a mixer with a lid, like a processor. This is great for adding flour and/or icing sugar while the motor is running, as it stops them flying around the room, but any good machine with beater and whisk attachments is fine. On occasion, the dough hooks are useful too. The advantage of a hand-held one is that you can use it when mixing things on the stove, for example the Easy American Frosting (page 92). If you put a single beater in, you can even whip cream in the carton.

PLASTIC OR PYREX MEASURING JUG

This is useful, not only for measuring liquids, but also for adding them gradually to the cake mix or pouring them over the finished cakes.

BAKING TINS

I've used good quality, non-stick tins throughout the book. You don't have to, but they'll make life easier and the results more predictable. Try to use roughly the same size as that given in the recipe, as a difference will inevitably affect the result.

SPATULA AND WOODEN SPOONS

A good spatula with a rubbery end can scrape almost every scrap of cake mix out of the bowl (in my day it was a wooden spoon or nothing, and a chance to lick the bowl clean of delicious raw cake mix). Wooden spoons still have their place, and I wouldn't be without my ancient but varied selection (including one inscribed with the wonderfully ghastly 'Nothing Beats the Archers').

NON-STICK SILICONE LINERS AND WORK SHEETS

Even though my pans are brilliantly non stick, I always slip a reusable liner into the bottom of each one when I bake, so that the cakes simply slip out of the tin. I have sheets cut to the size of every tray I have, so they're ready to use when I need them. For fruit cakes, sticky loaves and soaked cakes I use a specially 'slotted' liner, that lines the sides and bottom in one go: this not only makes them easy to remove from the tin and turn out, but saves wrapping the outside in extra paper for long-cooking fruit cakes, or wrapping the soaked cakes before pouring the liquid over them. I thoroughly recommend them. I also use a silicone sheet on my worktop if I'm kneading bread or rolling out icing, not only because it helps to stop them sticking, but also to make clearing up easier.
*See www.janeasher.com for special offer on silicone liners.

PASTRY BRUSH AND PIPING BAGS

A pastry brush is very useful for brushing the tin with oil or glazing the top of the cake with jam. Any good quality medium-sized brush is fine. It doesn't have to be a fancy cooking one – a paint brush will do well (preferably an unused one). Some disposable piping bags are useful for decoration.

RACK

You'll need one of these: cooling a cake on a rack stops the underneath getting soggy from the steam.

WEIGHING SCALES AND OVEN

Baking does require reasonable accuracy in terms of quantity and temperature, so it's worth having a decent pair of scales. (I have one of those electronic ones on which you use any container and add as you go or put back to zero and so on – and it weighs liquids too; I love it). If your results seem to be a bit odd, consistently, then check with a thermometer that your oven is more or less at the temperature it thinks it is; if not then you'll know to adjust it by the right amount each time. Most importantly, make sure you preheat the oven to the right temperature before putting in the cake.

PAPER CASES AND CUTTERS

If you're making fairy cakes, muffins or individual loaf cakes, paper cases are essential. You can find them in every kind of colour and pattern, including some pretty, metallic ones, which are great at Christmas time.

To make biscuits – or the Eccles cakes – you'll need some cutters, and it's worth buying good quality sharp ones in a set of different sizes, either fluted or plain rounds.

****

TO PREPARE THE CAKE TIN

If you use a reliable non-stick tin, simply brush the bottom and sides with a little vegetable oil and slip a re-usable silicone liner (or circle of baking parchment) of the right size in the bottom.

For especially sticky cakes, fruit cakes and soaked cakes, use one of the specially slotted liners that cover the sides and bottom in one, or cut a strip of baking paper for the side and a circle for the bottom.

If you are not using non-stick, or you're not sure it's in good condition, brush the inside of the tin with a little melted butter and then sprinkle it with flour (to be absolutely safe, you can chill the first layer of butter and then brush a second layer over it before flouring).

For proving breads and other yeast mixes: slip a slotted, round silicone liner into the bowl before putting in the dough – or oil the bowl lightly – to prevent sticking. Cover with a clean tea towel or cling film. *See www.janeasher.com for special offer on silicone liners.

STOCKISTS

You can get most of the equipment, chocolate, icings and decorations that I've used in the book by mail order from my sugarcraft store (www.janeasher.com) but many of them are also available in local shops or supermarkets.

If there's anything you need that you can't find elsewhere, then do e-mail me at the shop – info@janeasher.com – and I'll try to get hold of it for you. We love hearing about new products and ingredients and are always on the lookout for interesting developments in the world of baking!

INGREDIENTS

CHOCOLATE

It's really important to use the best quality chocolate. It doesn't necessarily have to have a very high cocoa solids percentage – in fact, for using in cake mixes or biscuits, if it's too high it will dry them out considerably. For baking, I'd recommend good Belgian dark chocolate chips with a cocoa solids percentage of about 50% and milk chocolate of about 33% (apart from the Squidgy Chocolate cake on page 39 which needs 70%+). The chips are much the easiest to use in cooking and decorating, as they melt very quickly and save you having to break up slabs of chocolate by hand. We can mail order them to you if you can't buy them locally (www.janeasher.com) .

For dipping, ganaches and other kinds of decoration, or when you want a really strong chocolate taste and texture, go for 70% or above of cocoa solids, also in chips form.

I melt my chocolate in the microwave: 100g takes about 2– 2½ minutes at full power, but you'll soon get to know. Or, of course, you can put the chips in a bowl over simmering water and melt them that way: just don't ever consider melting them directly in a saucepan, unless they're combined with something else, or you'll find yourself in trouble – chocolate is weird stuff and can suddenly turn on you and misbehave, becoming stiff, grainy and unusable.

COCOA POWDER

Never forget the wonderful, dense chocolate taste that good quality cocoa powder gives: a very simple way of adding chocolate to a recipe. Just an ordinary tub from the local shop – the same as you'd use for your bedtime drink – is what you want. Remember that it's entirely unsweetened, so there'll need to be some sugar somewhere else in the recipe. You'll need to sieve the cocoa powder as it can be lumpy.

FLOUR

As you'll see in my introductory 'masterclass' recipe for a Victoria Sandwich, I have experimented with many different types of flour while writing this book, and have come to some pretty definite conclusions: for cakes, it is worth buying the slightly more expensive self-raising flour that they call 'supreme' or 'premium' or whatever is the top-of-the-range flour made by a particular manufacturer. They genuinely don't need sieving – believe me, I've tried with and without and compared the amount of rising as well as done some 'family blind' tasting and there isn't the slightest difference. These high-quality flours, 'specially for cake making', have a lovely silky feel to them and are a delight to rub between your fingers (if you're into that sort of thing!). For the breads, crumpets and so on, or whenever I specify 'strong, bread flour', make sure you buy a good quality flour that mentions 'strong' on the packet; you can get Canadian strong bread flour that works very well.

FAT

I've tried all different kinds, from butter to margarine – both normal and softened – to oil-based spreads to white fat. I've definitely come down in favour of spreadable butter (there are plenty of different ones available). It's extremely easy to cream, you don't have to remember to get it out of the fridge ahead of time and I think the taste is just right. Because it has a percentage of vegetable oil mixed into it, it is less rich and heavy than butter alone, but still has a good buttery taste. Even for butter icing I now prefer it, so you can safely use it in all of the recipes (apart from a couple that need the fat to be rubbed into the flour, when it's better to use a cool block of butter, or half butter and half cooking fat, if you prefer). I use the slightly salted type of spreadable, which is traditionally incorrect, but as most cake recipes tell you to add a pinch of salt to the mix, I just leave that out and really can't see the difference. I even prefer the taste of butter icing with a hint of salt. Clearly, if you're on a low salt diet, you can use unsalted spreadable butter instead.

EGGS

These should be medium size for all the recipes and, for personal preference, I only ever use free range – not because of taste or for any other culinary reason, but simply because I don't want my food source (or its parent, in this case) to suffer before I eat it.

SUGAR

Ordinary white caster sugar is used in most of the recipes, but some need dark or light brown soft sugar, and occasionally I've used white granulated. Watch the lumps in the soft sugars; if your cupboard is at all damp, they can be quite hard, and you may need to break them up before using (or put the sugar in a bowl with a damp cloth over it for a while). Icing sugar will always need to be sieved.

LEMONS

The only thing to bear in mind is that, if the skin is to be used, the unwaxed ones are a good bet, although I've probably eaten plenty of wax in my time, before I realised it was on the skins.

VANILLA ESSENCE/EXTRACT

Don't even think about vanilla flavouring, which is pretty disgusting and bears very little relation to the real thing, even though the smell is, quite cleverly, close. An extract is the best, and although it costs a bit more than an essence it has a better, stronger flavour so you won't need to use much, and it'll last for a good long time.

VEGETABLE OIL

Any good quality sunflower, corn or rapeseed oil is fine. Although I'm an olive oil devotee, baking is one time when I don't use it, as it can be a little heavy and, even using one of the lighter ones, the taste can interfere with the cake or icing.

YEAST

If you're really into baking bread then maybe you have access to fresh yeast, but I must confess I haven't used it for years and for the purposes of this book the dried is fine. However, even if you use the new 'fast action' dried yeasts, I recommend that you don't follow their advice to put it straight into the flour, but activate it first in warm liquid as if it were the older type. I've tried both ways, and there's no question that the result is better if you do. It's a matter of moments, and in any case I love watching the yeast do its strange, creepy multiplying – like something from a horror movie. Any of the well known proprietary brands of dried yeast is fine, fast or not.

MALT

This can be quite hard to find nowadays (at least without added cod liver oil); I bought mine on line from www.herbsgardenshealth.com.

cakes

my perfect victoria sandwich

Experienced bakers can skip the detailed instructions for this recipe and not bother to look at the pictures, but for those just starting I hope this can work as a kind of 'master class' to give you the confidence to tackle the thousands of wonderful cake recipes from all over the world that begin in the same way. Over the years I've tried just about every combination of ingredients and methods for making what most of us call a 'sponge', and for the purposes of this book I went through it all again so that I could test some of the new fats and flours available.

(In fact, a true sponge cake contains no fat at all: it's fun to make if you have the patience – and makes you feel pretty smug when it works – as the lightness is achieved simply by warming the egg yolks and beating them like hell until they fluff up. The taste and texture can seem too insubstantial and a little dull on its own, although perfect for cakes like the Black Forest gateau (page 18) or Chocolate Swiss roll (page 70), which contain plenty of other fat in their fillings.)

This recipe is the culmination of all my attempts and is absolutely delicious and foolproof, and will make you feel happily proud as you set it down gently on the table for tea.

For quicker, simpler cakes for everyday teas, you can use the all-in-one method, with extra baking powder to achieve the lightness you would otherwise get from the initial creaming. As I dislike the faintly bitter taste this can give, I tend to use all-in-one recipes for flavoured traybakes (pages 24 and 33).

This traditional method of creaming the fat and sugar, and then adding the other ingredients in various stages, is a little slower than the all-in-one method, but it's only a matter of minutes and, with an electric mixer – which I thoroughly recommend – it's extremely simple to do. It only looks like a long process here because I've been so chatty and detailed for anyone doing it for the first time.

****

Victoria sandwich ingredients

4 medium eggs

the weight of the 4 eggs in:

spreadable butter (I like to use slightly-salted), caster sugar and premium, self-raising sponge flour (or 225 g of each)

1 teaspoon vanilla extract

a little water, as needed

Makes 10-12 slices

1 Pre-heat the oven to 180C (165°C fan assisted) 350°F, gas mark 4. Prepare two 20 cm sandwich tins (page 9). Put the butter and sugar into a large bowl and beat it hard with an electric mixer until it looks like whipped cream. Scrape any bits that escape – up the sides of the bowl or on to the beaters – back into the creamy mixture with a spatula, so that all of it is whipped up. Keep beating until the mixture is white – and when I say white, I mean really, really pale. You'll see it turn into a beautiful creaminess that is very different from the colour and texture of the original ingredients. This is an important stage – it's when you put all the lightness into your cake – and may take longer than you think; in my mixer, at high speed, it takes about 3-4 minutes.

2 Break the eggs into a cup, small bowl or, best of all, a small jug. Add the vanilla extract. Beat the mixture lightly with a fork to break up the egg yolks and to mix them with the whites. With the mixer motor running on full speed (or holding the handheld mixer in one hand), add the eggs very gradually to the butter/sugar mixture. This is almost like making mayonnaise – it's really worth taking time over it, as if you go too fast and the mixture curdles the finished texture just isn't quite right. After all, you're taking the trouble to make a beautiful home-made cake, so a little patience is well worth it at this stage.

3 Once all the eggs are in, add the flour (don't bother to sieve it), bit by bit. To do this by hand, sprinkle about a quarter of the flour on to the mixture and, with a spatula or large, metal spoon, fold it in. This means gently persuading it to mix in by turning the spoon as you scrape down the side and across the bottom of the bowl and up and over the top again. The idea is not to flatten out all that fluffy airiness that you've beaten into the fat, sugar and eggs. Repeat with the rest of the flour. This also works perfectly well in the mixer – either on slow speed or by using the pulse setting. I sprinkle it into the feed tube of my mixer, from the end of a spatula. The idea is to stop it landing in dollops on the creamy, eggy cake mixture, but instead to add it gradually and gently.

Notes on ingredients: *Although it's an old-fashioned idea, I found that weighing the eggs in the shells and then using the same weights of fat, sugar and flour for the mix gave me the perfect proportions, but if you don't have scales and are using a measuring cup or jug, then 225 g of each, to four eggs, will give good results. You can, of course, use all butter – or all margarine – but I found that spreadable butter was just the right half-way house: because it's made with oil it's lighter than butter, but has more taste than margarine (and is much easier to work with). I found the best flour to be one of the new 'supreme' sponge flours – and there's no need to sieve!*

4 Once all the flour is mixed in, take a spoonful of mixture and check the texture. It should drop gently off the spoon as you turn it upside down: if it doesn't, then add a tablespoon or so of water (I usually do). With the spatula or large spoon scoop half the mixture into each of the two sandwich tins, being as even as you can by eye, but again, not worrying about perfection (I have heard rumours of people weighing the two tins to check that they're exactly the same… hmmmm!). It may seem as if there isn't enough… but there is.

5 Bake for 25-35 minutes, in the centre of the oven, until they are well risen and golden brown. I recommend using a timer: you may think you'll remember that you have cakes in the oven but, if you're like me, it's only too easy to wander off and get involved in something else. Set the timer to the shorter of the two given times – in this case 25 minutes – and take a look. To check if they are cooked: either feel the tops with your finger – a robust 'springiness' is what you're after – or (probably safer if you're not sure) slide a sharp knife blade into the centre, down to the bottom, and check if there is any slimy uncooked mix on it when you pull it out (if this is the case, give them 2-3 minutes more and check again). If the knife comes out clean then you know they're done.

6 Check that they are not stuck to the tins, by sliding a small plastic spatula round the edge of each cake (or you may be able to see that they have already shrunken away from the side), then turn each one upside down, banging the edge of the tin on the worktop, if necessary, to dislodge the cake onto your other hand. Gently peel off the liner. Whichever cake has the better looking top should then be put on to a rack the right way up: the other one should be inverted so that what was the top flattens a little as it cools. Leave them to cool completely on the rack before decorating (see next page).

Three ways to decorate the Victoria sandwich

Classic

Once the cakes are completely cool, sandwich them together with a good layer of jam (and sweetened, whipped cream, for a treat – spread the jam on to one half and the whipped cream on to the other, before putting them together) then dust the top with caster sugar.

Charming retro

Sandwich the cake together with half a quantity of vanilla butter icing (page 90), then spread the rest over the top. Sprinkle with sugar strands or hundreds and thousands.

Strawberries and cream

Spread half of a quantity of sweetened, whipping cream (page 18) on to one cake, then slice a few strawberries fairly thinly and arrange them on top of the cream. Cover with the other cake. Spread the top with the remaining cream, then add the rest of the strawberries, either whole or halved, depending on size. Dust with a little extra sieved icing sugar. This is also delicious made with raspberries.

'delicious and foolproof...'

There's usually a good reason why certain dishes have remained popular over many years: a well made Black Forest gâteau is a treat. It's a classic, of course, and there have been many different versions since cherries, cream, Kirsch and chocolate cake were first put together in Germany nearly 100 years ago. I can't pretend my recipe is strictly accurate but, after much experimenting, I think this combination of ingredients is a winner – particularly the use of the slightly tart cherry compote rather than the more usual fresh or tinned fruit, as it stops the cake from being too sweet and keeps the taste of cherry zinging through.

black forest gateau

✳✳✳✳✳✳✳

6 medium eggs

200 g caster sugar

2 teaspoons vanilla extract

85 g plain flour

60 g cocoa powder, sifted

100 g butter, melted

For the filling and top

60 ml Kirsch (or use some juice from the cherries if you don't like liqueur)

450 ml double cream (or whipping cream if you like it slightly lighter)

2 tablespoons icing sugar

1 teaspoon vanilla extract

1 jar Bonne Maman cherry compote

grated chocolate, chocolate curls or vermicelli

1. Preheat the oven to 180°C (165°C fan assisted), 350°F, gas mark 4. Prepare three 20 cm sandwich tins (page 9). (You can bake in batches if you don't have three.)

2. In a large bowl, preferably with an electric mixer (if not, over a pan of simmering water), beat the eggs with the sugar and vanilla until pale and thick – for at least 5 minutes. With a spatula, gently fold in the flour and cocoa powder, then stir in the butter.

3. Divide the mixture evenly between the three tins, levelling the tops, then bake for 15-20 minutes, until the cakes are risen and springy and a knife inserted in the centre comes out clean. Allow them to cool for a couple of minutes in the tins, then turn out on to a rack to cool completely. Trim the sides neatly, so that they stack evenly.

4. Prick each cake all over with a fork, then sprinkle with the Kirsch or cherry juice. Pick out 12 of the best cherries from the compote then rest them on kitchen paper to dry a little (so they won't discolour the cream).

5. Whip the cream until it starts to thicken, then add the icing sugar and vanilla and beat again until it forms peaks. Don't overdo it. Spread one cake with just under a third of the cream then add spoonfuls of the compote, letting some of the liquid drain back into the jar. Use about half the jar. Repeat with a second cake then pile this on top of the first.

6. Add the final cake to the other two, then spread the top and sides with most of the remaining cream, keeping some back for decoration. Decorate the cake with piped swirls of cream, grated chocolate, chocolate curls or vermicelli. Add a little piped melted chocolate on top and a cherry to each slice.

****

125 g glacé cherries

200 g premium self raising flour

125 g spreadable butter

125 g caster sugar

4 medium eggs, lightly beaten

a little milk

Serves 8-10

A glacé cherry is as similar to a fresh cherry as a wooden bead is to a pearl, but, just like the beads, they have charm all of their own, and no self-respecting fruit cake should be without them. Cherry cake is a reassuringly old-fashioned tea time treat, but the version I make now looks different from the ones I remember. The reason is that I use naturally coloured glacé cherries - not only because it seems sensible to avoid artificial colours when there's a good alternative, but also because I love their deep red colour (although, as you can see, I ran out of them, so the cherries on top are the vivid scarlet ones of my youth).

cherry cake

1. Preheat the oven to 180°C (165°C fan assisted), 350°F, gas mark 4. Prepare a 900 g (21 x 10 x 6 cm deep) loaf tin (page 9).

2. Wash the glaze off the cherries with hot water, then dry well and cut each in half. Put the flour in a bowl and add the cherries to it, mixing them gently until they are well coated.

3. In a separate bowl, cream the butter with the sugar until very pale and fluffy, then add the eggs, beating them in well, a little at a time. Add the flour and cherries, with a little milk if necessary to reach a dropping consistency, and stir gently.

4. Spoon the mixture into the loaf tin, level the top, then make a slight dip in the centre.

5. Bake for 30 minutes, then reduce the oven temperature to 160°C (145°C fan assisted) 325°F, gas mark 3 and bake for a further 45 minutes, or until the cake is risen, golden and springy, and a knife inserted in the centre comes out clean.

6. Remove from the oven and allow the cake to cool for a couple of minutes in the tin, then turn out and transfer to a rack to cool completely.

Decorating ideas

This cake looks great served exactly as it is, or dusted with a little icing sugar. For a special tea, drizzle or ice the top with glacé icing (page 91) and decorate with a few glacé cherry halves.

I adore this quick, no-bake recipe, which, handily, uses up any leftover cake crumbs (it still works well if they're a bit stale), even though it has very little to recommend it nutritionally. I can't even claim it has the goodness of eggs included (no, the minuscule amount in the crumbs doesn't count). It's simply the most wonderful concoction of chocolate, sugar, butter and booze. But, hey, nutrition for the soul is just as important as it is for the body, and in that department this more than hits the spot.

chocolate fridge cake

1. Prepare a 20 cm square cake tin (page 9).

2. Put the chocolate, butter and golden syrup into a large, heatproof bowl set over a pan of simmering water and stir occasionally until all is melted together (or melt it in the microwave).

3. Take the pan off the heat and stir in the remaining ingredients.

4. Spoon the mixture into the prepared tin and chill until set (about 2-3 hours).

5. Cut into 9 or 16 squares.

Decorating ideas

This looks fabulous just dusted with a little sieved icing sugar, and I honestly think that if you added any icing or chocolate topping your sugar intake meter would implode . . .

For very special occasions it would look very elegant with a few scraps of gold leaf on top - or some gold almond dragées perhaps (ha! I knew I'd get some protein in there eventually).

350 g dark chocolate chips

125 g butter

2 tablespoons golden syrup

450 g cake crumbs

4 tablespoons brandy

225 g digestive biscuits, crushed

50 g glacé cherries, halved

Makes 9 large or 16 smaller portions (the smaller ones are plenty for most people!)

'nutrition for the soul'

chocolate traybake

This is a good example of using the all-in-one method of mixing, as the strong chocolate taste masks any hint of baking powder that might be picked up in a plainer cake. You needn't even sieve the cocoa powder – the mixer will get rid of any lumps. It's the perfect kind of traybake for school events, meetings of the local Druid group or whatever else, as it's extremely quick to make and wonderfully transportable if you leave it in the tray.

****

150 g self raising flour

1 rounded teaspoon baking powder

125 g caster sugar

125 g spreadable butter

3 medium eggs

35 g cocoa powder

Makes 10-12 portions

1. Preheat the oven to 180°C (165°C fan assisted), 350°F, gas mark 4. Prepare an 18 x 28 cm baking tin (page 9).

2. In a large mixing bowl, beat together the flour, baking powder, cocoa, sugar, eggs and butter until soft and blended, adding a little warm water as necessary to make a soft, dropping consistency.

3. Spoon the mixture into the prepared tin, smoothing evenly, and bake for 30-35 minutes, or until springy and a knife inserted in the centre comes out clean.

4. Allow to cool in the tin for a couple of minutes, then turn out on to a rack or, if you prefer, you can leave it to cool completely in the tin. Decorate with icing and cut into 10-12 slices.

Decorating ideas

This is most luscious topped with something chocolatey – you could either drizzle melted chocolate - dark, white or both – over the top or use chocolate butter icing (page 90). I've covered this one with chocolate ganache, used at pouring consistency (page 94) and sprinkled with a few crystallized rose petals.

Alternatively, you could use a sour cream icing (page 95) sprinkled with chocolate bits.

Clearly the Devil doesn't just have the best tunes but also one of the best cakes. I like to picture him, in magnificent scarlet, eating a huge slice of this classic dark, rich, decadent chocolate cake, tail twitching in delight. And I love the fact that it's his 'food' – I'm sure the Devil never tucks into anything as mundane or healthy as grilled fish or a bowl of porridge: it's chocolate or steak tartare all the way, I'll be bound.

devil's food cake

75 g spreadable butter

250 g light soft brown sugar

3 medium eggs, lightly beaten

100 g dark chocolate chips

175 g plain flour

2 teaspoons (10 ml) bicarbonate of soda

pinch of salt

185 ml milk

1 teaspoon vanilla extract

Makes 12-14 slices

1. Preheat the oven to 180°C (165°C fan assisted), 350°F, gas mark 4. Prepare two 20 cm sandwich tins (page 9).

2. Cream the butter and sugar together and beat well. This will have a strange texture – not pale and fluffy like usual creaming – because of the high proportion of sugar to butter. Then gradually add the egg, beating well all the time.

3. Melt the chocolate in a bowl set over hot water or in the microwave (about 2-2$\frac{1}{2}$ minutes on full power). Let it cool a little, then stir gently into the creamed mixture.

4. Combine the flour, bicarbonate and salt and add, gradually and gently, to the creamed mixture, alternating with the milk and vanilla (I use the pulse setting on my mixer).

5. Spoon into the sandwich tins, dividing it evenly, and smooth the tops. Bake for 30-35 minutes, or until the cakes are springy and a knife inserted in the centre comes out clean. Allow to cool for a couple of minutes in the tins, then turn out on to a rack to cool completely.

Decorating ideas

This is terrific filled with chocolate or vanilla butter cream and topped with chocolate fudge icing or chocolate frosting (page 94). Once you've sandwiched the two halves together with the butter cream, cover the sides and top completely with the icing or frosting, and then, with the handle of a spoon, or a palette knife, swirl it in lovely soft whorls - a bit like those horrible, badly-plastered ceilings. Or use a white frosting (page 92) – this is great for special occasions and looks fabulous with some sparkles or silver balls scattered on it.

****

100 g spreadable butter

100 g caster sugar

2 medium eggs, lightly beaten

1 teaspoon vanilla extract

100 g premium self raising flour

Makes 12 fairy cakes (or 24 mini ones)

Decorating ideas

Fine to eat just as they are, or you can dust them with a little sieved icing sugar. If you want to ice them, check that there's plenty of room between the top of each cake and the paper case. If not, just trim the rounded peak from each cake to make a flat surface, then flood with glacé icing or fairly liquid royal icing. Let them set a little before adding pretty decorations – either simple and classy *a la* Nigella, or go a little kitsch and wild and use some brightly coloured sprinkles.

Or you can pipe icing or ganache on to the tops – and decorate with all kinds of sweets, roll-out shapes or pieces of marshmallow.

For butterfly cakes (old-fashioned but very cute), slice the tops off the cakes and cut each slice in half. Spread the tops of the cakes with butter icing. Press the cut halves into it, angling them like wings.

fairy cakes

You might feel that the all-in-one mix, as used in the traybakes, would be good enough for cup cakes (or fairy cakes, as I'm calling them here, in homage to their original name). As with all food intended for children, I'm all for giving them as good a result as I would for adults and, as these are unflavoured and simple, I much prefer them without the faintly bitter taste that you can get from the baking powder used in the all-in-one method. And it really isn't much trouble to do it the 'proper' way: with an electric mixer it's purely a case of adding things bit by bit while the beater is whirring, rather than putting everything into the bowl to start with.

1. Preheat the oven to 190°C (175°C fan assisted), 375°F, gas mark 5. Place 12 paper cases (or 24 mini ones) into the moulds of a muffin or Yorkshire pudding tin – or on a baking tray. I like to use a muffin tin as it stops the cases losing their shape.

2. Cream the butter and sugar together until really pale and fluffy, then gradually add the egg, beating well all the time. Add about 1 dessertspoon of warm water and the vanilla.

3. Gently stir in the flour (or use the pulse setting on the mixer), adding it bit by bit.

4. Spoon the mixture evenly into the 12 paper cases and bake for 15-20 minutes (8-10 minutes for the mini ones), until the tops are golden. As they cook, they'll fill the cases.

5. Remove from the oven and let them cool in the paper cases.

'unflavoured and simple'

Sponge cakes, of course, are light and delicious, but sometimes I feel like a slice of old-fashioned Madeira, which has a little more body and says 'tea time' in a very English and satisfying way. Less fluffy than a sponge, it looks classically elegant, especially if topped with a drizzle of lemony icing. Plain flour, plus baking powder, gives the right texture for this, so for once you'll need to get the sieve out.

lemon madeira cake

✳✳✳✳✳✳✳✳

150 g spreadable butter

150 g caster sugar

4 medium eggs, lightly beaten

200 g plain sponge flour

1 teaspoon baking powder

grated zest of 1 unwaxed lemon

Makes 8-10 slices

1. Preheat the oven to 180°C (165°C fan assisted) 350°F, gas mark 4. Prepare a 15 cm diameter, deep cake tin (page 9).

2. Cream the butter and sugar together until light and fluffy – the mixture needs to be really pale in colour and considerably larger in volume before you go on.

3. Break the eggs into a small jug or large cup and beat lightly, before adding a little at a time, to the butter/sugar mixture, beating well after each addition.

4. Sift the flour and baking powder into a separate bowl, then fold gradually into the creamed mixture. Add the lemon zest and mix gently.

5. Spoon the mixture into the prepared tin and bake for 60-70 minutes until firm to the touch or until a knife inserted into the middle comes out clean. Let it cool for a couple of minutes in the tin, then turn out on to a rack and leave to cool completely.

Decorating ideas

This looks very good dusted with icing sugar and decorated with a few strands of lemon zest, but I also love it covered with lemon glacé icing (page 91) – a good use for the juice of the lemon, and decorated with some crystallised violets. Pour the icing over the cold cake, starting in the centre and allowing it to drizzle over the sides. When almost set, add the crystallised violets and place on a paper doily on a pretty plate.

'It says tea-time in a very English and satisfying way.'

lemon traybake

Another very easy traybake recipe: as far as I'm concerned you can't go wrong with lemon, one of my very favourite tastes, and it makes for a zingy, fresh cake that's great for summer teas or served with fruit as a dessert. As with the chocolate traybake recipe (page 22), you use the all-in-one method, which is quick to make – and to clear up.

✳✳✳✳✳✳✳

225 g spreadable butter

225 g caster sugar

4 medium eggs

300 g self raising cake flour

1 teaspoon baking powder

zest and juice of 1 large lemon

Makes 14-16 portions

1. Preheat the oven to 180°C (165°C fan assisted), 350°F, gas mark 4. Prepare a 30 x 23 cm baking tray (page 9). For deeper slices (as in the picture) use a 28 x 18 cm tray.

2. Simply put all the ingredients into a large mixing bowl and beat well together.

3. Spoon into the baking tray and bake for 35-40 minutes for the shallow cake and 40-45 minutes for the deeper one, until risen and springy to the touch. Let the cake cool in the tray.

Decorating ideas

1. Spread with lemony butter icing (page 90), mark into 16 pieces and decorate each one with a sugar 'lemon slice'.

2. Drizzle with lemon glacé icing (page 91) and, once it's set, cut into 16 pieces and top each portion with a slice of strawberry or with raspberries. Serve immediately, before the fruit 'melts' the icing.

'quick to make – and to clear up'

Most years I make my own marmalade, using the easiest, laziest method there is (the recipe is on my website), which I think makes for the best taste in any case. It's very satisfying packing it into jars and labelling it, although I'd be a non-starter in any W.I. competition: mine is poured into a wild assortment of containers, from those that held curry paste to huge dill pickle jars and Marmite pots, and would be disqualified immediately for not being presented correctly. Tastes great, though, so who's complaining? If I have any to spare, I make a steamed marmalade sponge (fabulous with custard) or this elegant cake, which is always a hit at tea time.

****

100 g spreadable butter

75 g caster sugar

2 medium eggs, lightly beaten

3 tablespoons marmalade

1-2 teaspoons orange zest

150 g premium self raising flour

2 tablespoons milk

1 teaspoon baking powder

Makes 8-10 slices

To make candied peel: score the peel of an orange into quarters and pull it away from the fruit. In a small pan, cover the peel with cold water, bring to the boil and simmer for 15 minutes. Drain, then repeat this twice. Drain and cool, then gently scrape away the white pith and cut the peel into strips. Boil 100g caster sugar with a little water until it reaches about 150°C, or 'thread'. Add the peel and cook for about 5 minutes. Drain, roll in caster sugar and leave to dry on baking parchment or silicon.

marmalade cake

1. Preheat the oven to 180°C (165°C fan assisted), 350°F, gas mark 4. Prepare an 18 cm cake tin (page 9).

2. Cream the butter and sugar together in a large bowl, beating until it is light, pale and fluffy (at least 3-4 minutes). Gradually add the egg, continuing to beat all the time.

3. Stir in the marmalade and orange zest. Mix the flour and baking powder together then fold into the cake mix, followed by enough milk to make a thick batter consistency. Spoon into the prepared tin and bake for 30-35 minutes, or until the top is golden brown and a knife inserted into the centre comes out clean.

4. Allow the cake to cool for a couple of minutes in the tin, then turn out on to a rack to cool completely.

Decorating ideas

For an everyday slice of cake with a cup of tea or coffee, just serve exactly as it is. For a special occasion – or if you love icing – a simple white glacé icing (page 91) drizzled or spread on top finishes it off, perhaps decorated with some candied orange peel (see left) or strewn with jelly 'orange slices'.

soaked lemon cake

I'm a great fan of lemon, as you may have noticed – there are three lemon recipes in the book – and used to eat raw slices of it when I was younger (not that I've gone off the idea, but only tend to do it now when I come across a piece lurking at the bottom of a gin and tonic). If your taste isn't for such sharp things, then this works equally well with orange juice. The soaking in syrup is the crucial bit, giving the cake its special, moist texture and fruity taste.

****

175 g spreadable butter

175 g caster sugar

3 medium eggs, lightly beaten

grated zest of 1 unwaxed lemon and the juice of 2 (about 3 tablespoons)

175 g premium self raising flour

pinch of salt

3 tablespoons milk

50 g granulated sugar

Makes 8-10 slices

1. Preheat the oven to 180°C (165°C fan assisted), 350°F, gas mark 4. Line the bottom and sides of a 900 g (21 x10 x 6 cm deep) loaf tin with baking parchment or a slit silicon liner (page 9) to come a couple of centimetres above the top edge.

2. Cream together the butter and caster sugar until really pale and fluffy, then gradually add the egg, beating well all the time. Add the zest, and gently fold in the flour and salt. Stir in the milk.

3. Turn the mixture into the prepared loaf tin and bake for about 35-45 minutes until springy to the touch and a knife inserted in the centre comes out clean. Remove from the oven but leave in the tin.

4. Put the granulated sugar and lemon juice in a small pan and bring to the boil, stirring all the time as the sugar dissolves. Boil strongly for about half a minute.

5. Make several holes in the cake with a skewer, going right to the bottom of the tin. Pour the hot syrup all over the cake, letting it seep into the holes. Leave to cool.

6. Holding the edges of the paper or silicon, carefully lift the cake out of the tin, then gently peel away the paper or liner.

Decorating ideas

You need something on top of the cake to hide the holes and, although a dusting of sieved icing sugar may be enough, it's very good drizzled with melted dark chocolate.

Try icing it with glacé icing (page 91) – either lemon or plain – and decorating with little candied lemon slices, or top with lemon butter icing, as I have here, then decorate with a twist of lemon rind.

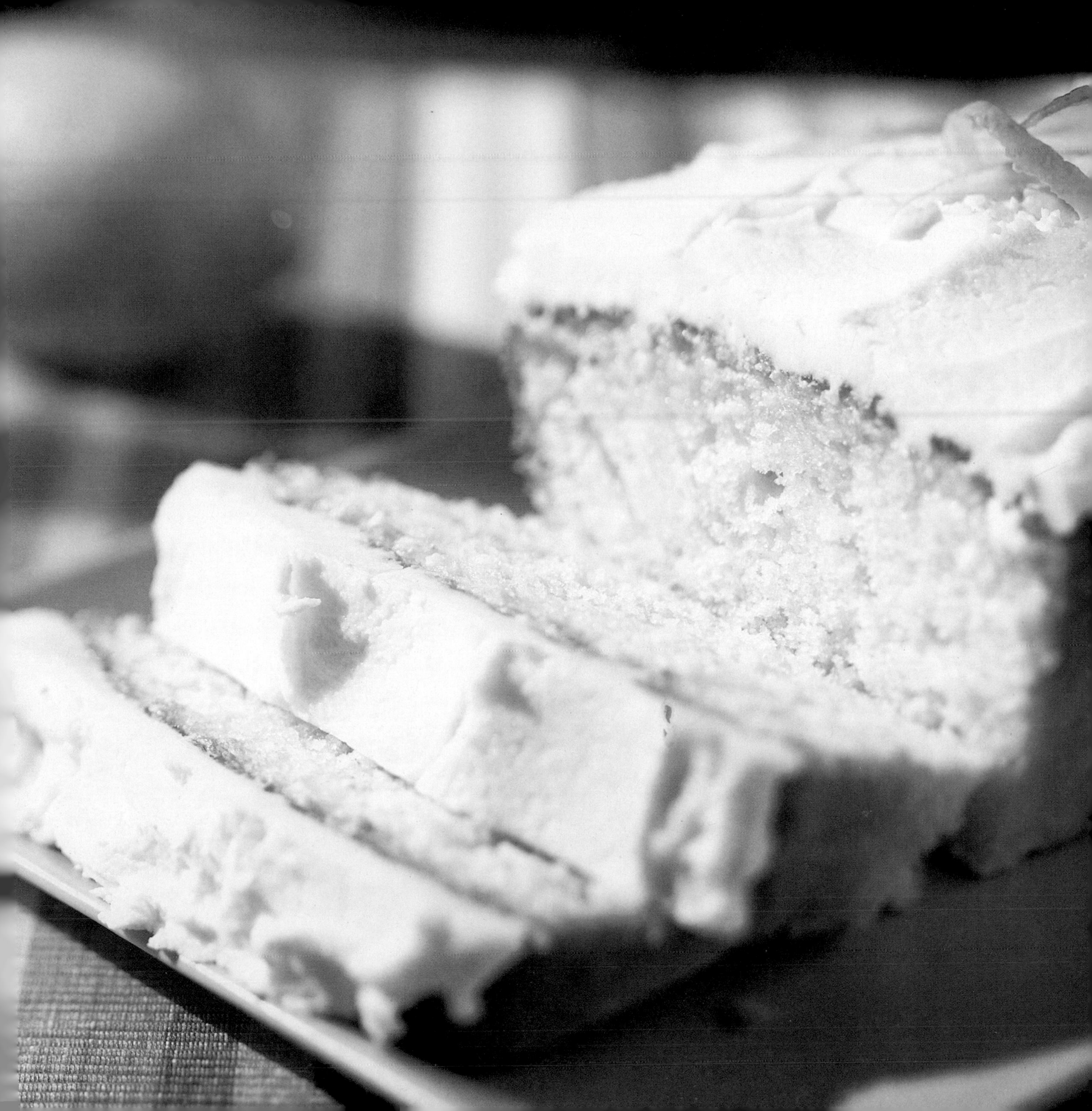

squidgy chocolate cake

This is a flourless cake that will collapse once out of the oven into a cracked, dense chocolatey delight – in a way it's a kind of soufflé, left to deflate and cool instead of being eaten hot and puffed up. Not difficult to make, it's one of my favourite cake recipes, and is guaranteed to please.

****

200 g dark, high cocoa content (70%+) chocolate chips

1 tablespoon brandy

1 tablespoon strong black coffee (made with good quality instant is fine)

150 g caster sugar

150 g butter

100 g ground almonds

5 medium eggs, separated

Makes a 20 cm cake, which – being very rich – will cut into 20-24 slices.

1. Preheat the oven to 180°C (165°C fan assisted), 350°F, gas mark 4. Prepare a deep 20 cm round cake tin (page 9, and for this recipe flour as well as grease the tin or, preferably, use a liner).

2. Put the chocolate chips, brandy, coffee, sugar and butter into a large, heatproof bowl and melt together, either in the microwave or over a pan of hot water. Stir well until it becomes smooth. Allow to cool a little, then stir in the ground almonds, followed by the egg yolks, one by one.

3. In a large bowl, beat the egg whites until stiff, then stir gently into the chocolate mixture.

4. Spoon the mixture into the cake tin and bake for 35-45 minutes, depending on how squidgy you like it. Let it cool a little in the tin, then turn out on to a rack to cool completely.

Decorating ideas

This cake looks fabulous simply dusted with a little sieved icing sugar, but, for special occasions, try topping it with some gold almond dragées, or even with a few flakes of real gold leaf and some cocoa powder. (As you can see, I've gone a little mad here and covered the top with gold leaf, which I've then rubbed away a little to make it look 'antiqued'). Serve the cake on its own or with fresh raspberries, accompanied by dollops of crème fraîche, whipped cream or mascarpone.

'dense chocolatey delight'

tres leches cake

****

175 g spreadable butter

175 g caster sugar

3 medium eggs, lightly beaten

175 g premium self raising flour

175 ml evaporated milk

125 ml (about 100 g) condensed milk

100 ml double cream

Makes 8-10 slices

I've adapted this from a wonderful Mexican recipe, which has also been popular in Texas for many years. Although it's really more of a pudding than a cake, it's so delicious that I couldn't resist including it. The principle is that of a soaked cake, like the lemon one on page 34, but instead of a syrup, the cooked cake is soaked in three different types of milk, hence the name. For a cake that includes all that cream and condensed milk, it's surprisingly light, and looks rather angelic in its white innocence, especially if you cover it with fluffy white frosting. Remember that, as it includes all that dairy produce, you'll need to keep it in the fridge when not eating it.

1. Pre-heat the oven to 180°C (165°C fan assisted), 350°F, gas mark 4. Prepare a 900 g (21 x 10 x 6 cm deep) loaf tin, lining it with baking parchment or a shaped silicon liner (page 9) to come well above the sides of the tin.

2. Cream the butter and sugar together, beating well until really pale and fluffy, then gradully add the egg, beating well all the time.

3. Gently fold in the flour, then stir in 3 tablespoons of the evaporated milk. Turn the mixture into the prepared loaf tin.

4. Bake for about 40-50 minutes, until springy to the touch and a knife inserted in the centre comes out clean. Remove from the oven but leave in the tin.

5. Make several holes in the cake with a skewer, going right to the bottom of the tin.

6. While the cake cools for 10 minutes or so, mix the remaining evaporated milk with the condensed milk and cream in a jug.

7. Pour the creamy milk mixture over the cake, squashing the top a little and encouraging it to seep into the holes. (You may have to do this bit by bit, waiting after each addition for a few minutes while the liquid soaks in). Refrigerate for at least an hour – preferably more like four hours, or even overnight.

8. Carefully lift the cake from the tin, by holding the edges of the paper or silicon, then gently peel away the paper or liner.

Decorating ideas

The traditional finish is to cover the cake with sweetened whipped cream, sometimes decorated with pieces of fruit, but my favourite is to use American frosting (page 91), which has such a beautiful texture and whiteness to it. Finish by scattering it with a little edible glitter for a really snowy, sparkling centrepiece.

jane's last-minute christmas cake

Traditionally, a Christmas cake should be made months ahead of the Great Day, to give it time to mature in taste and texture. But don't worry: this recipe is perfect if you've forgotten (or been too busy) to make it ahead of time. The heating and soaking of the fruit in the boozy liquid, plus using dark brown sugar, gives an overnight appearance of maturity . . . I think it's a delicious recipe to use even if you are making it early, and it's my favourite for our family Christmas cake.

****

750 g mixed dried fruit

150 g glacé cherries

225 ml Guinness

100 ml whisky

75 ml orange juice

zest of 1 orange

2 tablespoons black treacle

4 medium eggs, beaten

200 g spreadable butter

200 g soft brown muscovado sugar

250 g plain flour

1 heaped teaspoon (7 ml) baking powder

1½ teaspoons mixed spice

75 g chopped Brazil nuts or almonds

Makes 30-35 small portions

1. Place the dried fruit, cherries, Guinness, whisky, orange juice, zest and treacle in a large saucepan and bring to the boil, stirring. Simmer gently for 10 minutes, then remove from the heat and allow to cool completely. Preferably, transfer to a bowl and refrigerate overnight - but don't worry if you can't, just leave it soaking as long as you can.

2. Preheat the oven to 140°C (125°C fan assisted), 275°F, gas mark 2. Lightly grease a 20 cm round deep cake tin and line with baking parchment or a shaped silicone sheet (page 9).

3. In a mixing bowl, place the remaining ingredients, except for the nuts, and mix thoroughly (I did mine in the electric mixer because I was feeling lazy). Beat until smooth, then fold in the soaked fruit and the nuts. Spoon into the prepared tin and level the top, making a slight dip in the centre. Bake for 3 hours, then take a look: cover the top with more paper or silicone if it is over-browning. Bake for a further ½-1 hour, or until a knife inserted in the centre comes out clean. Allow to cool for 10 minutes or so in the tin, then turn out and allow to cool completely on a rack.

4. When completely cool, wrap the cake in baking parchment and then in foil, and store in a tin somewhere cool and dry (oh, for the days of larders!) until it's time to decorate it. Every couple of weeks (or more often, if you're short of time), unwrap the cake, make a few holes in the top with a skewer, and spoon over a little brandy or whisky. This keeps the cake moist – and makes it taste even better. You can use orange juice if you prefer. If you like really moist cake with no 'crust', then leave the cake in the tin when it comes out of the oven and feed it with the alcohol in that.

To cover with marzipan

If you like marzipan, you need to put it on to the cake a couple of days before you ice it – just to make sure that the oil in the marzipan doesn't seep into the icing. (If you use white marzipan, it's less likely to discolour the surface, especially if you use roll-out icing, rather than royal.) You can make your own marzipan, but the packets of white are so good that you may feel, as I do, that your time is better spent elsewhere at this hectic time of year.

1. With a sharp, serrated knife, trim the top of the cake if necessary, and turn it upside down, to give a flat surface.

2. Knead 450 g white marzipan well until soft. Roll it out on a work surface (or silicon sheet) dusted with a little icing sugar, to a circle large enough to cover the whole cake. Brush the cake with a little sieved apricot jam. Roll up the marzipan onto the pin, then unroll it to drape over the cake. Smooth the marzipan with your hands until it covers the cake evenly, then trim away any excess from the bottom edge.

3. Wrap the cake loosely in baking parchment and leave for a day or so before decorating.

Decorating ideas

Well, clearly, when it comes to decorating a Christmas Cake there are as many alternatives as there are... robins on Yule logs. It's such a busy time of year that, unless you're feeling particularly keen, it's a good opportunity to make use of ready-made icings and decorations, and there are plenty of beautiful ideas around in magazines, books and websites. As this is a baking, rather than decorating, book, I'll restrain my natural impulse to tell you how to turn your cake into an igloo or a cracker, and simply give you this elegant, extremely easy way of making it into a fabulous, natural-looking centrepiece. This is perfect for those who don't like icing – the decoration just goes straight on to the marzipan, and the centrepiece is mounted on its own little board, and so can be taken off and put on the table once the cake is cut. You can keep it from year to year – just replacing the fruit and candles as necessary. If you like icing, then you can easily use the same centrepiece on a white, iced cake.

1. Using the glue gun (or a tube of glue) stick the candle on to the cake board then, with more glue, add the other decorations, tying the twigs into a little bunch with raffia. (If you like, you can gild the physalis with a little gold leaf – just pull back the dry leaves and press them gently on to the gold leaf. I've also gilded a couple of the walnuts).

2. Position the decoration in the centre of the cake. Add extra bay leaves to hide the edge of the board. Tie more raffia around the outside of the cake in a knot and trim stray strands, as necessary, with scissors.

****

1 white or cream candle

selection of nuts in their shells, mandarins or clementines, physalis, cranberries, bay leaves etc.

gold leaf (optional)

glittery twigs etc.

glue gun or tube of glue

1 x 4 mm thin, 13 mm cake board

length of raffia

truly last-minute do-not-panic christmas cake!

If you've completely forgotten to make a Christmas cake, keep calm. As long as you can find a corner shop or supermarket open and buy yourself a ready-made cake then all is not lost, and you can produce something that will look very pretty and may well pass for home made. This uses jam, sweets and ribbon (the kind of things you may well have sitting round the house at Christmas time), and can be achieved in minutes.

1. Buy a ready-made fruit cake – the best you can find. Make loads of holes in the top with a cocktail stick and pour a little brandy or whisky over until it soaks in (or use orange juice if you don't like alcohol). This will help to make the cake moist, as well as tastier than it might have been.

2. Brush the top with jam (preferably light-coloured and sieved, but whatever you've got will do), then arrange sweets, glacé fruits, shelled nuts, glacé cherries, etc. in lines, circles, or however you fancy, on top.

3. Put a couple of dollops of jam into a small pan, add a little more whisky, brandy or fruit juice and warm slightly to make it runnier. Brush it all over the sweets, etc. and leave for a few minutes to set slightly.

4. Tie a beautiful ribbon around the side and add a bow.

'achieved in minutes and can pass for home made...'

biscuits

ginger nuts

Nowadays anything with 'nuts' in the title is asking for sniggers, but in my childhood the name of this much-loved biscuit was a frequent term of endearment – or, on occasion, abuse – for redheads like me, along with other equally risqué terms, such as 'copper knob'. I'd probably be able to sue for harassment today, but I confess that I always rather enjoyed it: the reminder that I was part of a minority, someone different from the norm, with an interesting recessive gene, almost made up for the horrifying freckles, invisible eyelashes and pale, itchy, sensitive skin. So, on behalf of all my fellow carrot tops, I just had to include this recipe. Sam, the photographer, ate the lot, so they must taste good too.

✳✳✳✳✳✳✳✳

50 g butter

125 g golden syrup (4 generous tablespoons)

50 g dark soft brown sugar

175 g self raising flour

1 teaspoon cinnamon

2 teaspoons ground ginger

Makes 12-14 large or 24 small biscuits

1. Preheat the oven to 180°C (165°C fan assisted), 350°F, gas mark 4. Prepare a large baking tray (page 9).

2. In a small saucepan, melt together the butter, syrup and sugar, stirring.

3. Combine the flour and spices in a large mixing bowl and make a well in the centre. Pour in the melted sugar/butter mix and stir with a wooden spoon until it comes together as a dough.

4. Divide the dough into 24 small pieces (or 12 for large biscuits) and roll each into a ball. Place on the tray and flatten each very slightly with your finger (they will spread in the oven).

5. Bake for 8-10 minutes, or until starting to brown, then remove from the oven and allow to cool for a couple of minutes before transferring to a rack to cool completely.

Decorating ideas

Best served just as they are: crisp, spicy and warming. But you could always glaze them with a little white icing and gold leaf, if you fancied tarting them up a bit (all ginger nuts enjoy dressing up now and then).

These are good biscuits to make if you can't be bothered to get out the rolling pin and cutters, or to chill and slice the dough – simply pile up the mixture using a spoon and sprinkle some flaked almonds on top. Think of it, in film terms, as the equivalent of cinéma vérité: a little rough, perhaps, but with immense character and integrity. I was thinking of calling them almond piles, but thought better of it... The almond taste is very subtle (the way I like it). If you prefer it more dominant, simply use almond extract instead of the vanilla.

almond cookies

****

125 g spreadable butter

65 g granulated sugar

$\frac{1}{2}$ teaspoon vanilla extract

1 medium egg, lightly beaten

125 g plain flour

50 g ground almonds

few flaked almonds (about 10-15 g)

caster sugar, for dusting

Makes 10-12

1. Preheat the oven to 180°C (165°C fan assisted), 350°F, gas mark 4. Prepare a large baking tray (page 9).

2. Cream the butter and sugar together and beat until light and fluffy.

3. Add the egg very gradually, beating all the time, then beat in the vanilla extract.

4. Mix in the flour and ground almonds, either with a spoon or on slow speed in the electric mixer then, using a dessertspoon, scoop little piles of the mixture on to the tray. Press a few flaked almonds on top of each (yes, some will – maddeningly – drop on to the tray: don't bother to pick them out. How clever of you to make some toasted, flaked almonds ready to decorate your trifle or whatever…).

5. Bake the cookies for 15-20 minutes until golden brown. Remove from the oven and sprinkle with a little caster sugar. Let them cool for a couple of minutes on the tray, then move to a rack to cool completely.

'immense character and integrity'

****

shortbread

There are loads of different shortbread recipes – and it's very much a matter of personal taste as to how crumbly it should be: this version, with a little cornflour added, is just the way I like it. Although you can shape and cut it any way you fancy, I love the look of 'petticoat tails,' which is what the divided round is known as in Scotland. It's traditional to add the markings before you bake the shortbread, but I find they show up much better if you add them as soon as the shortbread comes out of the oven. Don't just eat it with tea or coffee – it's perfect with a glass of wine or champagne.

****

100 g spreadable butter

50 g caster sugar

150 g plain flour

25 g cornflour

Makes 8-10 pieces

Decorating ideas

I prefer shortbread plain, but if you're keen on chocolate then it's very easy to melt a few good quality milk or plain chocolate chips in the microwave and, with the tip of a fork or piping bag, drizzle the chocolate over the shortbread. (This works well on straight-sided shapes – press the dough into a large rectangle and mark into eight sections before baking). Allow the chocolate to set for a while in a cool place.

1. Preheat the oven to 165°C (150°C fan assisted), 325°F, gas mark 3. Prepare a baking tray (page 9).

2. Using a wooden spoon, cream the butter and sugar together in a mixing bowl until pale and creamy.

3. Sift together the flour and cornflour and add to the creamed mixture, encouraging it to blend in with the back of the spoon.

4. Turn out the dough (even if it's still in separate lumps) on to a work surface or silicon sheet dusted with flour, and work it gently with your hands until it comes together (don't overdo it or the dough will become oily and tough).

5. Put the dough on to the baking tray and press it with your knuckles into a round, about 20 cm across, gently squashing and encouraging it into shape, making it as even as you can (but the homemade look is attractive – so don't worry too much). If you want your circle perfect, then an easy way is to put a greased flan ring (or side of a loose-bottomed cake tin) on to the baking sheet and press the dough into it. Once the shortbread is evenly pressed to the edge all round, just lift off the ring. Score gently with a knife four times, marking the shape into eight pieces.

6. Bake for 25-30 minutes, or until the edge is just beginning to turn golden brown. Remove from the oven and, with the handle of a teaspoon, flute around the outside edge. Use a fork to decorate with little holes then cut gently into eight pieces while still warm and soft. Sprinkle with a little extra caster sugar while still warm.

oatmeal, raisin and chocolate cookies

Most of the recipes in this book are my personal variations on fairly traditional British ones, but these delicious cookies are more in the modern American style. They are as different to the thinner British biscuit as the grey, flat, meat patties of my childhood were to the genuine thick, juicy hamburgers that came over from the US in the 70s. Not that I don't, on occasion, have a certain fondness for a Rich Tea biscuit with a cup of tea, even though it's a world away from chewy, rich, dense cookies, like these ones below.

****

100 g spreadable butter

100 g light soft brown sugar

50 g caster sugar

1 teaspoon dark 'runny' honey

1 medium egg, lightly beaten

1 tablespoon milk

125 g self-raising flour

1/2 teaspoon baking powder

1/2 teaspoon bicarbonate of soda

1/2 teaspoon ground cinnamon

175 g medium oatmeal

125 g raisins

125 g white Belgian chocolate chips (or milk or plain, to taste)

Makes about 18 cookies

1. Preheat the oven to 190°C (175°C fan assisted), 375°F, gas mark 5. Prepare two baking trays (page 9).

2. Cream the butter, sugars and honey together, beating well until the mixture is really pale and fluffy. Gradually add the egg and milk, continuing to beat well.

3. Combine the flour, baking powder, bicarbonate of soda and cinnamon, then fold gently into the creamed mixture (or use pulse on the mixer).

4. Stir in the oatmeal, raisins and chocolate – it looks as if it won't come together at first, but it will. Using a spoon, put little piles on to the baking trays, using your hands to bunch the mixture together, if necessary. The cookies will spread and flatten as they cook. Bake for 10-12 minutes, until just starting to colour round the edges – no more, if you like them as chewy as I do. Don't panic! They will seem very mushy and soft as you take them out of the oven.

5. Allow them to cool on the trays for a few minutes, just until they are firm enough for you to move them gently on to a rack to cool completely – if you can bear to wait that long to eat them.

Decorating ideas

These are best left well alone – although for very special occasions you could always drizzle with a little extra chocolate or white royal icing (page 92).

These biscuits have a dense, almost bitter, taste and suit those seriously into chocolate. If you decorated them really prettily, you could even make them to give as presents, nestling in little boxes tied with ribbon. They're very quick to make and the dough cuts beautifully. Try using shaped cutters for special celebrations: at Christmas you could always make a little hole in each one with a straw before cooking and, once cooled and decorated, thread them with ribbon to hang on the tree.

quick chocolate biscuits

1. Preheat the oven to 200°C (185°C fan assisted), 400°F, gas mark 6. Prepare a large baking tray (page 9).

2. Place all the ingredients in the bowl of an electric mixer and blend for a few seconds on slow speed, then turn the speed to high and beat well until the mixture comes together as a stiff dough.

3. Turn out on to a work surface or silicon sheet dusted with icing sugar and knead briefly until the dough is smooth. Roll out gently, with a pin dusted with icing sugar, to a depth of about 1 cm. Cut shapes with a sharp cutter – this amount will make about 14-16 rounds of 5 cm in diameter.

4. Place the biscuits on the baking tray and bake for 8-10 minutes, until set and just beginning to rise a little (they will harden as they cool). Allow to cool a little on the tray, then transfer to a rack to cool completely.

Decorating ideas

The biscuits are tasty just as they are, although a little dry for some tastes. They're very good simply piped with a little melted white or dark chocolate, or dipped half into chocolate ganache or glacé icing.

✳✳✳✳✳✳✳✳

50 g spreadable butter

50 g light brown soft sugar

150 g self raising flour

30 g cocoa powder

2 generous tablespoons black treacle or molasses

2 medium egg yolks

icing sugar for rolling

Makes 14-16

'give as presents, nestling in little boxes'

nutty coconut bars

Coconut is a bit like Marmite – you either love it or hate it (I'm in the positive camp for both). This is a quick to make, very moreish recipe that makes the most of coconut's distinctive taste and interestingly chewy texture. Thank goodness, convenience-wise, desiccated coconut is one of those relatively rare ingredients that, when used in certain recipes, tastes better than fresh: much as I adore cracking open and eating a coconut straight from the fair (or supermarket) there's no doubt that, in baking, grated, real coconut just doesn't work.

****

100 g plain flour

75 g cold butter

30 g caster sugar

2 medium eggs

100 g soft light brown sugar

pinch salt

175 g desiccated coconut

50 g each chopped almonds and walnuts

Makes 10 generous bars

1. Preheat the oven to 190°C (175°C fan assisted), 375°F, gas mark 5. Prepare a 20 x 10 cm baking tray (page 9).

2. Put the flour into a large bowl and rub in the butter with your fingertips until the mixture resembles breadcrumbs. Stir in the caster sugar, then press into the prepared tin and bake for 15 minutes.

3. Meanwhile, beat the eggs in a bowl with the brown sugar. Add the salt, coconut and nuts and mix well. Spread this over the base and bake for a further 20 minutes.

4. Allow to cool for a few minutes in the tin, then turn out on to a rack to cool completely before slicing, with a sharp, serrated knife, into 10 bars.

Decorating ideas

Before slicing, drizzle the top of the cake with lemon glacé icing (page 90) or melted plain chocolate.

'interestingly chewy texture'

simple lemon or vanilla biscuits

****

125 g spreadable butter

150 g caster sugar

1 medium egg yolk

225 g plain flour

zest of 1 lemon or $^1/2$ teaspoon
vanilla extract

makes 12-14 biscuits

This basic, roll-out biscuit dough makes delicious, classic biscuits. I make them in my food mixer, but you could do them by hand as long as you beat the sugar and butter really well together before adding the egg. They're great just dusted with a little caster sugar and served plain with stewed fruit or fruit salad, but are also delicious topped with icing for special treats.

1. Preheat the oven to 180°C (165°C fan assisted), 350°F, gas mark 4. Prepare two large baking trays (page 9).

2. Cream together the butter and sugar very thoroughly until pale and fluffy. Gradually add the egg yolk, together with the vanilla, if using, beating well as you do so. Stir in the flour and zest (for lemon biscuits) and keep mixing until it begins to come together as a dough, then tip it out on to the work surface or silicon sheet lightly dusted with flour and knead lightly with your hands.

3. Roll out the dough to about 5 mm thick, then cut out rounds or shapes. Place on the baking trays, allowing a bit of space for them to spread, and bake for about 15 minutes until just beginning to turn pale brown. (Don't worry if they seem soft – they'll harden as they cool).

4. Remove from the oven and allow to cool for a couple of minutes before transferring to a rack. Dust them lightly with caster sugar and leave to cool completely.

Decorating ideas

1. Spread with a little lemon glacé icing (page 91) and decorate with sprinkles.

2. Substitute 3 level tablespoons of cocoa for the same amount of flour in the biscuit recipe. Sandwich the cooked biscuits together in pairs with a little chocolate butter icing. Spread a little extra icing on the top and add some chocolate sprinkles.

3. Spread differently coloured glacé icings on to animal-shaped biscuits. Add piped details with a small amount of royal icing and add silver balls for eyes etc.

chocolate caramel shortbread

Well, if you will buy a baking book you can't expect tofu and soya beans, can you? This is a pretty indefensible recipe, and I wouldn't advise putting it in children's lunchboxes too often, or their chances of supermodel stardom are, unlike them, going to be slim. These are for treats only, since not only do they contain the delicious trio of fat, sugar and chocolate, but also one of my own favourites: condensed milk. (My father used to say that perfection would be to lie in a hot bath drinking condensed milk from the tin – shame he's no longer around: imagine how easy it would be to fulfil this admirable dream now that it comes in a squeezy bottle.)

****

180 g spreadable butter

75 g caster sugar

200 g plain flour

25 g soft brown sugar

450 g can (or squeezy bottle) condensed milk

200 g milk chocolate chips

Makes 10-12 very filling slices

1. Preheat the oven to 180°C (165°C fan assisted), 350°F, gas mark 4. Prepare a 28 x 18 cm baking tin (page 9).

2. Put 150 g of the butter into a bowl, together with the caster sugar and, using a wooden spoon, cream together until soft. Add the flour, mixing it into the creamed mixture with the back of the spoon.

3. Turn out into the prepared tin, spreading and pressing it out evenly with your hand, then bake for 30-35 minutes until just beginning to colour at the edges. Remove from the oven and allow to cool in the tin.

4. Put the remaining butter, brown sugar and condensed milk in a small pan and heat gently, stirring, until it begins to bubble. Keep scraping the bottom, or it will burn (although don't worry about a few dark bits – they'll soon be covered in chocolate!).

5. Continue to stir until the mix thickens - this will only take a couple of minutes – then remove from the heat and, still stirring, let it cool for a few seconds, before spreading it over the shortbread base. Allow to cool.

6. Melt the chocolate in a basin set over hot water or in the microwave, then spread it evenly over the caramel. Leave the chocolate to set, then cut into rectangles.

Decorating ideas

Are you kidding? The only thing to add to this is to go for a run.

macaroons

What makes these macaroons especially tasty and 'almondy', without being bitter, is the use of a high quality extract, rather than the fake flavourings that I remember from my childhood. These are very easy and quick to make, and a good use of any left over egg white (rather than making meringues yet again). I did use a piping bag to put mine on the baking tray, as I had one easily to hand, but spoonfuls would be just as good, if not quite as evenly circular. If you don't have any rice paper, you could put these on to baking parchment or silicon, but the edible paper is half the fun, I think.

****

1 medium egg white

50 g ground almonds

100 g caster sugar

$1/2$ teaspoon almond extract

1 packet rice paper sheets

few flaked almonds

Makes 8-10

1. Preheat the oven to 180°C (165°C fan assisted), 350°F, gas mark 4. Put the rice paper sheets on to a large baking tray.

2. Whisk the egg white until stiff, then fold in the ground almonds, sugar and almond extract (the texture will be a bit strange, but that's as it should be).

3. Pipe (with a plain nozzle) or spoon 8-10 round shapes on to the paper. (Give left-over sheets of rice paper to any nearby children, for writing secret, edible messages to each other with food colour pens — unmissable fun.) Top each one with a flake of almond.

4. Bake for 20-25 minutes, until just beginning to turn a caramel colour. Remove from the oven and cool on a rack, then trim away any surplus rice paper with scissors.

Decorating ideas

Best left well alone, I think, although the ubiquitous dusting of icing sugar wouldn't do any harm.

'the edible paper is half the fun'

bakes

This delicious gingerbread – a cake, not the kind of gingerbread that you make men out of, which is more like a biscuit – is very easy to make and not overpoweringly spicy (add more ginger if you like it strong). It's a wonderful alternative to Christmas cake, if you decorate it dramatically, or is a treat with a cup of tea anytime.

gingerbread

1. Preheat the oven to 170°C (155°C fan assisted), 325°F, gas mark 3. Prepare an 18 cm square cake tin (page 9).

2. In a small pan, heat the treacle, syrup, sugar and butter until everything is melted and blended. Set aside to cool a little.

3. Combine the flour, salt, ginger, cinnamon, ground cloves, baking powder and bicarbonate in a large bowl, sieving the spices if they look lumpy. Add the almonds and sultanas and make a well in the centre.

4. Add the egg and milk to the melted treacle, then pour into the dry ingredients, mixing slowly at first and then thoroughly until it becomes a smooth batter.

5. Pour into the prepared tin and bake for about 1 hour. Remove from the oven, allow to cool for a few minutes in the tin, then turn out on to a rack to cool completely.

Decorating ideas
Mediaeval Gold

This is wonderful at Christmas time, or for a Golden Wedding party, perhaps. I was inspired to use the gold when the phrase 'that takes the gilt off the gingerbread' came into my head. Don't ask me why . . .

Drizzle, Jackson-Pollock-style, with glacé or soured cream icing (page 91) then decorate with gilded almonds or slices of ginger (simply press each dampened nut or slice of ginger on to gold leaf until it picks up enough to look pretty). Cut the gingerbread into 9 squares and add an almond or ginger slice to each piece. Or use gold dragees, as I have here.

Or top the gingerbread with vanilla or orange butter icing (page 90).

✳✳✳✳✳✳✳✳

3 tablespoons black treacle

2 tablespoons golden syrup

125 g dark brown soft sugar

85 g butter or margarine

225 g self raising flour

1/2 teaspoon salt

1 tablespoon ground ginger

1 teaspoon cinnamon

1/2 teaspoon ground cloves

1 teaspoon baking powder

1/2 teaspoon bicarbonate of soda

30 g flaked almonds

50 g sultanas

1 medium egg, beaten

125 ml milk

Makes 9 large or 16 small squares

foolproof meringues

I can't absolutely guarantee that these won't let you down, as the success of meringues appears to be one of those things that's subject to the phases of the moon, or your bio-rhythms, or the fact that there are 13 spoons in your drawer. However, if you use the chef's trick of adding a tiny bit of vinegar to the beaten egg whites then I can promise you a near certainty of producing beautiful, elegant, perfectly textured meringues (terms and conditions apply . . . please see small print before suing me). And I don't even bother to fold in half the sugar – I've experimented for this book and they turn out just as well if you mix it all in at once.

****

egg whites from 2 medium eggs

100 g caster sugar

1 teaspoon white wine vinegar

Makes 7-8 large ones or 10-12 small ones

1. Preheat the oven to 125°C (110°C fan assisted), 230°F, gas mark ¼. Line a baking tray with baking parchment or a silicon sheet.

2. Whip the egg whites until very stiff. Add the sugar and vinegar and whisk again, until it's almost as stiff as before (don't worry, you won't taste the vinegar once they're cooked, even though you can smell it now and you're feeling very uneasy).

3. Put generous dessertspoonfuls on to the baking tray (or pipe through a large nozzle).

4. Bake for about 3 hours, depending on how chewy you like them. (If you want them really white, you can bake them at an even lower temperature, though I prefer them to have a hint of colour, with slightly chewy centres, unlike the shop-bought, ultra-white ones that shatter at a touch.) Remove from the oven and cool on a rack.

Decorating ideas

Classically, these would be sandwiched together with some whipped cream - and that's pretty hard to beat (the idea, not the cream). You'll need about 140 ml to fill this amount of meringues. For special occasions, serve them with fresh strawberries or raspberries or - one of my favourites – some sweetened chestnut purée. You could even really go to town and add a little silver leaf to the tops or drizzle with chocolate.

Meringues are also wonderful crumbled up and mixed with whipped cream and smashed strawberries – a pud that goes under the wonderfully English name of 'Eton Mess'.

banana muffins

There are some natural essences and extracts that work very well in recipes – for example, vanilla or chocolate – but, for my taste, banana just has to be fresh. Luckily there always seem to be a couple of them beginning to go black and squishy in our fruit bowl, and recipes like this are perfect for using them up.

  Muffins are not only very tasty and comforting, they are also one of the easiest cakes to make, as a certain lumpiness in the original mix is an essential part of getting the right consistency; too much beating and hard work and they'll have a rubbery, uneven texture.

****

250 g self raising flour

150 g caster sugar

75 g fine oatmeal

2 large, ripe bananas

2 medium eggs, lightly beaten

50 ml oil

150 ml milk

Makes 12 muffins

1. Preheat the oven to 200°C (185 °C fan assisted), 400°F, gas mark 6. Put 12 paper cases into a muffin tin.

2. Put the flour, sugar and oatmeal in a large mixing bowl and make a well in the centre.

3. In another bowl, mash the bananas with a fork (or a potato masher works brilliantly) and stir in the eggs, oil and milk.

4. Add the banana mixture to the flour and stir briefly with a wooden spoon until just combined but still lumpy - this will feel weird, but keep calm. Don't over beat.

5. Spoon the mixture into the muffin cases and bake for 15-20 minutes or until golden brown

6. Let the muffins cool for a minute or two in the tin, then transfer to a rack to cool completely.

Decorating ideas

These are perfect served just as they are, warm from the oven, perhaps with a dollop of crème fraîche on the side, or split and spread with butter.

To make a delicious topping: cream 120 g cream cheese together with 2-3 tablespoons icing sugar and 1 dessertspoonful of lemon juice. Spread over the muffins and finish with chocolate sprinkles Or drizzle with orange glacé icing (page 91).

american brownies

A brownie is to a slice of chocolate cake what rock 'n' roll is to jazz: just as satisfying in its own way, but with a more accessible, younger feel that, at the right time, hits the spot perfectly. Brownies were invented – just as rock 'n' roll was – in the US, and this simple but wonderfully dense and chewy recipe reminds me of the brownies I used to eat warm with vanilla ice cream in Joe Allen's restaurant in New York.

****

200 ml vegetable oil

150 g golden granulated sugar

100 g dark brown soft sugar

2 teaspoons vanilla extract

3 medium eggs

60 g cocoa powder

100 g self raising flour

$1/4$ teaspoon salt

$1/4$ teaspoon sodium bicarbonate

100 g chopped hazelnuts or walnuts (optional)

Makes 10 generous brownies

1. Preheat the oven to 180°C (165°C fan assisted), 350°F, gas mark 4. Prepare a 20 x 25 cm (or 23 cm square) baking tin (page 9).

2. Put all the ingredients into a large mixing bowl and beat well together.

3. Spoon the mixture into the prepared tin and bake for 25-30 minutes, depending on how chewy you like your brownies (I take them out when the centre is just set, but not yet firm).

4. Let the brownies cool in the tin (unless you want to eat them warm), then turn out and decorate.

Decorating ideas

You can simply serve the brownies sprinkled with a little sieved icing sugar. Alternatively, cover them with chocolate butter icing or chocolate frosting (page 94), then decorate with nuts or chocolate drops. For very special occasions, they look fantastic with a few gold dragees or edible glitter on top. Serve with a dollop of crème fraiche, whipped cream or ice cream.

'eat warm with vanilla ice cream'

****

3 medium eggs

65 g light brown soft sugar

50 g plain flour

2 heaped tablespoons cocoa powder

caster sugar for dusting

Makes 8-10 slices

Decorating ideas

You need a light filling that's easy to spread, as this cake is delicate and fluffy and would break easily. As the cake is pretty sweet, it's delicious with tangy sour cream icing, which is beautifully sloppy and easy to spread when just made, but firms up perfectly as it sets. Simply melt 100 g dark chocolate chips in a basin set over hot water (or in the microwave) and stir in 200 ml of sour cream. Beat well and if the mix doesn't seem smooth and melted enough to spread then reheat a little in the microwave or over hot water. Once the Swiss roll is spread with the filling, chill it to firm up.

Alternatively, use a chocolate or vanilla butter icing (page 90) with a little hot water added, or whipped cream, flavoured with vanilla and sugar (pictured) – and I so love the look of some caster sugar dusted sparklingly on the almost perfect surface (sigh!).

chocolate swiss roll

My home-made Swiss rolls nearly always crack – but then I think that's what stops them looking like shop-bought ones, and any serious disasters can always be hidden with a little chocolate icing... I've experimented with many different methods of rolling them up, and, after much trial and error I think the following way is the best hope of success.

1. Preheat the oven to 200°C (185°C fan assisted), 375°F, gas mark 7.

2. Cut two sheets of baking parchment measuring about 37 x 46 cm. Butter one of the pieces and place it on a baking tray measuring 33 x 23 cm inside (the paper won't sit in it, of course, just lie on the top; don't worry, the mix will weigh it down later).

3. Put the eggs and sugar in a bowl and beat well on high speed for 5- 8 minutes until the mixture is really thick, pale and fluffy. Sift the flour and cocoa powder together, then gently stir into the mixture until blended, then spread it over the buttered paper, smoothing the top evenly and encouraging the paper down into the baking tray - don't worry if the edges aren't perfect, as you'll trim them later. Bake for 8-10 minutes until just set – don't overcook! I found 8 minutes was enough in my oven.

4. Meanwhile, have ready a large silicon sheet (or tea towel, although I find the silicon easier), the other sheet of baking parchment and the caster sugar. Remove the cake from the oven and sprinkle the top with sugar. Cover with the baking parchment, then the silicon sheet (or tea towel), and invert everything carefully on to the work surface.

5. Carefully lift one short end of what is now the upper paper away from the cake just a little – about 3-4 cm – and score a line across the cake, cutting just half way into it. Replace the paper. This helps the initial bend as you roll. Now roll up the cake, together with both the inner and outer sheets of paper and the tea towel or silicon sheet.

6. Allow to cool for about 10 minutes, then, very carefully, unroll the cake and gently remove the inner paper. Leave to cool again, while you make the filling.

7. Spread with the filling, then trim the edges neatly with a very sharp knife. Re-roll, without the outer paper. Dust with a little extra caster sugar if necessary. Glory in your triumph, or get the chocolate icing out if you need to cover a disaster.

I'm not getting deeply into pastry in this book (sounds a bit uncomfortable anyway) as there just isn't the space to do it justice. But I'm including these (a particular favourite of my husband's), as they are clearly cakes, not pies, and very quick and easy to do. They are made with flaky pastry, which I always buy ready-made – either fresh or frozen. I never make my own anymore (unlike shortcrust) as it's tricky and time-consuming: I feel about it rather as I do about calculators and long division – it's interesting and fun to do it a few times and understand the principle, but after that the quick (and, in my case, better) way out is entirely justifiable...

eccles cakes

1. Preheat the oven to 220°C (205°C fan assisted, 425°F, gas mark 7). Melt the butter in a small pan, or in the microwave, then add the fruit and nutmeg. Prepare a large baking tray (page 9).

2. On a lightly floured work surface or silicon sheet, roll out the pastry to about 15 mm thick and cut out large circles (about 100 mm in diameter). Re-roll left over pastry as necessary until you've cut 8-10 circles.

3. Damp the edge of each pastry circle with water, and put a couple of teaspoons of the filling into the centre of each. Draw up the edges to the middle, enclosing the filling in little 'pouches'. Pinch the edges to seal then trim away as much of the excess pastry as possible, or you'll end up with very thick bottoms to the cakes. Lightly flour the surface again and invert the cakes on to it, so that the joins are underneath. Roll out each cake very gently until they are flattened slightly and the currants just begin to show through the pastry.

4. Make two slashes in the tops with a sharp knife (or one… or three… opinion varies as to the traditionally correct number!), then brush with a little milk and sprinkle with caster sugar. Place on the baking tray.

5. Bake for 15-20 minutes until golden brown, then transfer to a rack to cool, sprinkling with a little extra sugar if desired.

****

40 g butter

75 g currants

50 g mixed peel

pinch nutmeg

450 g flaky pastry

caster sugar, for dusting

Makes 10-12

new york cheesecake

My first experience of really good cheesecake was in a New York deli when I was 20 – touring the US in Shakespeare – and, cheesecake-wise, I've never looked back. Although there are many different types, for me it always has to be the baked, creamy American kind that has a texture all its own.

****

For the crust

100 g digestive biscuits (7 biscuits), put in a strong plastic food bag and bashed with a rolling pin to make crumbs

35 g butter, melted

1 heaped tablespoon Demerara sugar

pinch of ground cinnamon

For the filling

750 g cream cheese

225 g caster sugar

4 medium eggs, plus 1 egg yolk, lightly beaten

1 heaped tablespoon plain flour

50 ml double cream

1 teaspoon vanilla extract

1 dessertspoon lemon juice

1 heaped teaspoon lemon zest

1 heaped teaspoon orange zest

For the topping

320 ml soured cream

1/2 teaspoon vanilla extract

1 heaped tablespoon granulated sugar

Feeds 16-24 people, depending how you slice it!

1. Preheat the oven to 220°C (205° fan assisted), 425°F, gas mark 7. Prepare a 23 cm springform cake tin (page 9).

2. Combine the crumbs, butter, sugar and cinnamon in a large bowl, then press into the bottom of the tin. Chill in the fridge while you make the filling.

3. Cream the cheese and sugar, beating well. Gradually add the egg, continuing to beat well. Stir in the flour, then the cream, vanilla, lemon juice and zest.

4. Pour into the prepared tin and bake for 15 minutes, then reduce the heat to 110°C (95°C fan assisted), 225°F, gas mark 1/4) and bake for a further 45-55 minutes, until set but not browned. Don't over cook at this stage – the cake shouldn't rise up at the sides or begin to show cracks!

5. Meanwhile, prepare the topping by mixing together the soured cream, vanilla and sugar in a small bowl.

6. Remove the cake from the oven and raise the temperature to 180°C (165°C fan assisted), 350°F, gas mark 4. Spread the topping over the cake and return it to the oven to bake for a further 5-10 minutes until set but not colouring.

7. Remove from the oven and put immediately into the fridge to chill overnight. Carefully remove the outside ring before serving. It's easier to leave the cheesecake on the base.

Decorating ideas

To make a beautiful dessert, top it with fruit. Make a simple glaze by gently heating about 115 g apricot jam in a small saucepan with a little water. Pass it through a sieve, then keep warm over a low heat until you're ready to use it, thinning it with water as necessary. My favourite topping is blueberry: simply wash 2 small or 1 large punnet of fresh blueberries, paint the top of the cheesecake with glaze, then arrange the blueberries on top. Paint more glaze over the berries, then chill to set.

cheese and walnut loaf

This is much lighter than a traditional wholemeal walnut bread and is very good spread with butter to accompany soup, but it's also surprisingly good with cheese, as the relatively small amount of cheddar in the bread complements, rather than fights, the taste of whatever cheese you eat with it. If you want to serve it with a delicate soft cheese, you could add some raisins or sultanas and forget the cheddar. I've made mine a round cob shape, but you can just as well make it in a loaf tin: full size or individual ones.

****

150 ml tepid milk

1 teaspoon caster sugar

1 ½ teaspoons dried yeast

450 g strong white bread flour

1 teaspoon salt

140 g strong cheddar cheese, coarsely grated

75 g walnuts, chopped

25 g butter, melted

175 ml tepid water

Makes 12-14 slices

1. Stir the sugar into the warm milk, then sprinkle the yeast on top. Leave for 5 minutes or so to froth up.

2. Put the flour, salt, cheese and walnuts into a large mixing bowl. Make a well in the centre, add the butter and water, and stir with a wooden spoon, or your hand, until the mix comes together as a dough.

3. Turn out the dough on to a lightly dusted work surface (or silicon sheet) and knead for about 10 minutes, until springy and elastic.

4. Put into a clean bowl, either lined with a slotted silicon circle or lightly oiled to prevent sticking, and cover. Leave to rise in a warm place until almost doubled in size (for about an hour).

5. Knead again briefly, and either put into a 900 g (21 x10 x 6 cm) loaf tin or shape and place on a baking tray. Cover and leave to rise again until doubled in size. Meanwhile, preheat the oven to 230°C (215°C fan assisted), 450°F, gas mark 8.

6. Bake for 30-40 minutes, until well risen and beginning to brown on top. Remove from the oven, cool in the tin for a few minutes, then turn out on to a rack to cool completely.

Decorating ideas

For a shinier top, brush the loaf with a little beaten egg before baking, then, if liked, sprinkle with some kibbled wheat or sesame seeds.

malted fruit loaf

This is a lovely, old-fashioned bread that is great with a cup of tea or coffee, spread with butter, or just to pick at during the day, and is lighter than the densely sticky type you buy ready made. Malt reminds me of my childhood – I used to be given a spoonful of it every now and then for some supposed health benefits, but as I adored the taste it was no hardship. You need to find a jar of pure malt (page 11) – don't even think of trying to make it with the malt you can buy mixed with cod liver oil, which is disgusting.

****

1 teaspoon caster sugar

75 ml warm water

$1/2$ level teaspoon (7 g) dried yeast

2 tablespoons malt

1 tablespoon black treacle

10 g butter

225 g plain flour

$1/2$ teaspoon salt

100 g raisins

Makes 8-10 slices

1. Prepare a 900 g (21 x 10 x 6 cm deep) loaf tin (page 9).

2. Dissolve the sugar in the warm water and sprinkle the yeast on top. Leave for 5 minutes or so until foamy.

3. In a small pan, melt together the malt, treacle and butter (if you think you know stickiness, you ain't seen nothing till you've worked with malt . . .).

4. Put the flour, salt and raisins into a large bowl, make a well in the centre and pour in the yeast and malt mixtures, stirring with a wooden spoon until it comes together into a dough, adding a little extra water, as necessary, to bring it together.

5. Turn out on to a lightly floured work surface or silicon sheet and knead for 5 minutes or so until the dough is firm and springy. Shape into an oblong, fold to fit into the loaf tin, and leave in a warm place for about 1$1/2$ hours until well risen - it should pretty much fill the tin.

6. Bake for 30-40 minutes in an oven preheated to 200°C (185°C fan assisted), 400°F, gas mark 6. Cool in the tin for a few minutes, then turn out on to a rack to cool completely (or enjoy a slice while it's still warm – delicious!).

Decorating ideas

The loaf looks and tastes fine just as it is, sliced and buttered. If you fancy a shinier finish, though, it's very easy to glaze the top: mix a dessertspoonful of sugar into the same amount of water and brush it over the loaf when it comes out of the oven.

crumpets

Well, of course, shop-bought crumpets are perfectly good, and, once toasted, I couldn't honestly swear that these will taste dramatically different or better. But they are such fun to make, and you feel so clever when those bubbles come to the top of the mixture and burst – creating those cute little butter-soaking holes - that I thoroughly recommend trying it at least once. If you can grab some nearby children, let them help you: this is one of those recipes that demonstrates the magic of yeast and the wonder of applying heat to a few simple ingredients, and may well inspire a love of cooking (and, hopefully, science) that will last them a lifetime. Although the joy of melted butter alone is hard to beat, I also love them with Marmite, jam or peanut butter.

****

450 g strong white bread flour

1 teaspoon caster sugar

1 teaspoon salt

2 level teaspoons 'easy-blend' or 'fast-action' dried yeast

560 ml warm milk

140 ml warm water

Makes about 14-16

You'll need some crumpet rings to make these: they're worth buying as making crumpets any other way just doesn't look right, and they're quite useful for little flans and things afterwards (well, maybe not that useful, but they're not very expensive).

1. Put the flour, salt, sugar and yeast into a large mixing bowl and make a well in the centre. Add the warm milk and water and gradually mix it into the flour with a wooden spoon. Once most of it is absorbed, beat well until it becomes a smooth batter.

2. Cover the bowl with cling film or a cloth, and leave in a warm place until the mixture has almost doubled in size (this will take about an hour).

3. With a little butter or oil, grease a large, thick-bottomed frying pan and the crumpet rings, then put the rings in the pan and place the pan on a medium heat. After a minute or so, pour batter into each ring to about halfway up. Cook for about 5 minutes, turning down the heat if you think the bottoms may be over-browning, until bubbles come to the surface and burst (wow!).

4. Remove the rings and turn over the crumpets to cook on the other side for a couple of minutes. Repeat until all the batter is used up.

5. Once they're cool, pop them in the toaster until golden brown on the 'holey' side, then serve hot, spread with butter.

Scones are worth making yourself not only because they'll always be that bit fresher than shop bought but also because they are so quick and simple. There are loads of different recipes – some add egg to the mix, for example, and others glaze the tops before baking, but this one makes them exactly the way I like them: the texture is light and slightly crumbly and they taste fabulous with or without the fruit. Eat them fresh the day you make them, preferably warm from the oven, with the traditional cream and jam, or, if you have some left over the next day, split and toast them and serve with butter.

perfect scones

****

225 g self raising flour

¼ teaspoon bicarbonate of soda

pinch of salt

50 g cool butter, not spreadable in this case, cut into small pieces

25 g caster sugar

50 g of one of the following: currants, raisins, sultanas or mixed fruit (optional)

150 ml milk

Makes 10-12

1. Preheat the oven to 220°C (205°C fan assisted), 425°F, gas mark 7, and put a large baking tray in to get hot (no need to grease or line it).

2. Mix together the flour, salt and bicarbonate in a bowl (sifting if there are any lumps) and rub in the butter until the mixture resembles breadcrumbs.

3. Stir in the sugar and the fruit, if using. Make a well in the centre and stir in enough of the milk to give a fairly soft dough. Turn out on to a floured work surface or silicon sheet and, if necessary, knead very lightly, just to remove any cracks.

4. Roll out very gently (or pat out with your hand) to a thickness of about 2 cm, then cut out rounds with a 6 cm cutter. Sprinkle the tops with a little extra flour and place on the hot baking sheet.

5. Bake for 10-12 minutes, or until well risen and the tops are golden brown. Cool on a rack (or eat them warm!) and serve split and buttered, or with whipped cream and strawberry jam.

'light and slightly crumbly'

These are so simple that they are great to make with children. Little drop scones (or 'dot coms', as they've delightfully come to be called in Hugh Fearnley-Whittingstall's family) are a tea time favourite, with or without the fruit, and far easier for little ones to cook than full-blown pancakes. Proper pancakes are very fragile and can easily end in tears - and tears, if you see what I mean (ah, the quirks of English pronunciation!). They're much tastier than the shop-bought ones, which have a texture a bit like rubber gaskets (ok, I admit - even the best home-made ones have a hint of gasket, but only of the highest quality rubber).

sultana drop scones

****

225 g plain flour

pinch of salt

5 ml spoonful each of bicarbonate of soda and cream of tartar

100 g caster sugar

1 medium egg, lightly beaten

200 ml milk

50-75 g sultanas

small amount of butter for frying

Makes 10-12

1. In a large bowl, mix together the flour, salt, bicarbonate of soda and cream of tartar (sifting if there are any lumps). Add the sugar and mix well.

2. Make a well in the centre and pour in the egg and about a quarter of the milk, stirring with a wooden spoon (or use a hand-held blender) and letting the flour mixture fall into the centre as it's gradually blended.

3. Continue adding the milk and stirring until you have a thick, smooth batter. Stir in the sultanas.

4. Heat a large, flat frying pan (or a griddle, if you have one) and melt a tiny piece of butter, spreading it around the pan with a brush or spatula, until the whole surface is greased and slightly bubbling.

5. Drop spoonfuls of batter on to the hot pan (I find I can fit four into my large pan) to make small scones. After about a minute, or when bubbles are bursting on the top, turn over the scones and cook on the other side, again for about a minute. Add a little extra butter to the pan between each batch, as necessary.

Serving ideas

Serve the scones warm, spread with a little butter. Or sprinkle with lemon juice and dust with caster sugar. Once cold, you can always lightly toast them to perk them up a bit.

Baking bread can be wonderfully simple nowadays, thanks to bread machines, which, for everyday loaves, are terrific. Also, of course, in the last few years good bread has become more readily available on the high street. So, if you are going to take the trouble – and have the immense pleasure – of making your own, I think it's worth choosing something a bit special, like this beautiful and delicious sweet brioche. This is wonderful eaten on its own, very fresh, or with butter and jam – or toasted to serve with pâtés and terrines.

sweet brioche

****

25 ml warm water

50 g caster sugar

1½ level teaspoons dried yeast

50 g caster sugar

225 g strong white bread flour

pinch of salt

50 g butter, melted and allowed to cool slightly

2 medium eggs, lightly beaten

beaten egg mixed with a little water for glazing

Makes 8-10 slices or 9 individual loaves

1. Prepare a baking tray (page 9) or put individual paper loaf cases in a tin.

2. Pour the water into a cup or small bowl and stir in 1 teaspoon of the sugar. Sprinkle the yeast on top and leave it for 5 minutes or so until frothy.

3. In a large bowl, combine the flour, salt and remaining sugar. Add the yeast liquid, the melted butter and the beaten egg to the flour and mix well until it comes together into a dough. Turn out on to a floured work surface or silicon sheet and knead for 5 minutes or so until springy and firm.

4. Put the dough into an oiled polythene bag, or a bowl lined with silicon and covered with cling film (page 9). Leave in a warm place for 1-2 hours, until doubled in size.

5. Turn out the dough on to the work surface again and divide into three. Roll, squeeze and encourage each piece into a longish sausage shape - it'll try hard to spring back! With a little water, stick the three pieces together at one end, and then plait them carefully, bringing the outside piece into the middle alternately. Stick the ends together when you can't go any further. Alternatively, divide the dough into nine and put into the paper cases.

6. Carefully place on the baking tray and cover with oiled clingfilm (or put into a large, oiled plastic bag). Leave in a warm place again for another hour or so until well risen. Meanwhile, preheat the oven to 220°C (205°C fan assisted), 425°F, gas mark 7.

7. Brush the top of the plait or loaves with the egg wash and bake (15-20 minutes for the plait or 10-15 minutes for the loaves) until the top is golden brown. Remove from the oven, allow to cool for a minute or two then transfer to a rack to cool completely.

These are more like breads than cakes, and are particularly good split, toasted and spread with butter and jam. Of course you can buy similar at a reasonable price, but never anything quite as fresh. You can make them exactly the way you like: choose from raisins, currants, sultanas, with or without peel, for instance, or try some chopped apricots or cranberries. If you store them in an airtight container, they'll keep for a few days, or they freeze beautifully.

tea cakes

****

200 ml warm milk

1 tablespoon caster sugar, plus 1 teaspoon

2 level teaspoons dried yeast

450 g strong white bread flour

1 teaspoon salt

75 g mixed dried fruit

25 g melted butter

a little warm water

1 medium egg, lightly beaten

Makes 4-6 large tea cakes

1. In a cup or small bowl, stir the sugar into the warm milk, then sprinkle the dried yeast on the top. Leave for 5 minutes or so until foamy.

2. In a large mixing bowl, mix the salt into the flour. Stir in the fruit, then add the yeasty milk, the warm water, melted butter and the egg. Mix well until it comes together into a dough. Scoop on to a work surface dusted with flour or covered with a silicone sheet and knead well - you don't have to keep going as long as for bread, just until the dough is smooth and springy.

3. Place in a clean bowl, either lightly oiled or lined with silicone, cover with cling film or a cloth and leave in a warm place for an hour or so until doubled in size.

4. Divide the dough into four or six and shape into round buns. Place on a prepared baking tray (page 9) and leave in a warm place to prove for a second time, until the oven heats . Meanwhile, preheat the oven to 220°C (205°C fan assisted), 425°F, gas mark 7.

5. Bake for 15-20 minutes until they are springy to the touch and beautifully risen. Allow to cool for a few minutes then transfer to a rack to cool – or eat while still warm . . .

Decorating ideas

For a shiny, sticky finish, mix a dessertspoonful of caster sugar with the same amount of water and stir until the sugar is dissolved. Brush over the hot tea cakes as they come out of the oven. Or put the tea cakes on a rack over some paper, to catch the excess, then drizzle with glacé icing to make iced buns.

easy banana, walnut and peanut butter loaf

Okay, I'll come clean, I've cheated with this title. I was determined to include a peanut butter recipe in the book, just because I love it so much. I tried incorporating it into all kinds of things, from cookies to breads and cakes, but when I included enough to get the full 'hit' of peanut taste, the texture was really weird and dense, and when I was more subtle, I achieved the perfect texture but lost the taste. So, I've come to a momentous decision: it's better to add the gorgeous stuff afterwards, either via my newly invented peanut butter butter icing (I love writing that), or just as it comes out of the jar. These loaves are sensational spread with either, and the combination of flavours is terrific.

****

2 medium eggs

3-4 very ripe bananas

125 g caster sugar

120 g spreadable butter

225 g self raising flour

1 teaspoon baking powder

3 tablespoons sour cream

75 g walnut pieces

Makes a 900 g loaf, or 9 individual loaves

1. Preheat the oven to 180°C (165°C fan assisted), 350°F, gas mark 4. Line a 900 g (21 x 10 x 6 cm deep) loaf tin with paper or silicon (page 9), or line individual shapes with paper loaf cases.

2. Put everything, except the walnuts, into a large mixing bowl and beat with an electric mixer on high speed until smooth and blended together. Stir in the walnuts (if your electric mixer is pretty tough you can add these with everything else).

3. Tip the mixture into the tin or paper cases and bake for 60-65 minutes (20-25 minutes for individual loaves), or until a knife inserted in the centre comes out clean.

4. Remove from the oven and lift the loaf out of the tin by holding the edges of the paper or silicon. Carefully peel away the paper or silicon and allow the loaf to cool on a rack (or eat a slice warm!). Serve the individual loaves in their cases.

Decorating ideas

Offer slices with a bowl of peanut butter or peanut butter butter icing (page 90). Or you could slice the loaf in half and sandwich it together with the peanut butter butter icing.

icings

butter icing

Perfect for filling and/or topping almost any kind of cake.
Traditionally you're meant to use unsalted butter, but I much
prefer it with the touch of salt that you get in slightly salted,
'spreadable' butter, which I prefer to use for cakes as well, because
of its lighter texture and marginally less fatty ingredients.

Put the butter and sieved icing sugar (yes, I know I say you hardly ever need to sieve in cake-making, but for this you may well have to or you may get lumps) into a mixing bowl and beat together. I do it in my mixer, with the lid on, which stops the icing sugar flying about, but you can do it with a fork or with a hand-held electric mixer if you take it slowly. Add a few drops of warm water to soften the icing if necessary, and keep beating until the mixture gets really light and fluffy.

Chocolate butter icing

Replace 50 g of the sugar with 50 g of cocoa powder.

Vanilla butter icing

Guess what? Leave out the warm water and add a few drops ($\frac{1}{2}$ teaspoon or so) of vanilla extract…

Orange or lemon butter icing

Leave out the water and add a little grated rind of the fruit and a couple of teaspoons of the juice (beat well while you add it, or it may curdle).

Coffee butter cream

Melt 2 teaspoons of strong instant coffee granules in a little hot water, let it cool and add to the icing instead of the warm water.

****

enough to fill and top (or cover completely, without filling) an 18-20 cm round cake.

100 g spreadable butter

200 g icing sugar

warm water

peanut butter butter icing

This is my own invention, as the White Knight would have said, and surprisingly good – it may seem strange to put sugar with a spread that we think of as savoury, but, after all, we make loads of sweet and nut combinations, from walnut cakes to peanut brittle. Adding the butter improves the texture and taste at the same time.

Beat together the peanut butter with the icing sugar and butter, adding a little warm water as necessary to make it smooth and creamy.

****

enough to top or fill an 18-20 cm round cake

50 g peanut butter (smooth or crunchy, to taste)

50 g sieved icing sugar

25 g spreadable butter

glacé icing

The simplest icing of all, and very handy for drizzling or for quickly covering fairy cakes and so on.

Simply sieve 150 g icing sugar into a bowl and gradually add 1-2 tablespoons warm water (be careful! don't overdo it or you'll have to add more sugar… then more water… then more sugar – like cutting legs off a table and never getting it even). Beat well. It should be thick enough to coat the back of a spoon.

For a classier, slightly glossier icing, warm it in a little saucepan – but don't let it get too hot (you can heat it in a bowl set over simmering water, if you want to be sure of it).

It's easy to flavour glacé icing, by substituting fruit juice, dissolved cocoa or strong coffee for the water.

****

enough to cover an 18-20 cm round cake or 16-18 fairy cakes

royal icing

Another very simple, classic icing that can be used to cover large cakes, drizzle on to smaller ones or biscuits, and for piping, if you want to get fancy.

****

enough to cover an 20-23 cm round cake, or 18-20 fairy cakes

1 medium egg white
175-225 g sieved icing sugar, depending on the consistency you're after…

Whisk the egg white lightly in a largish bowl until it's well broken up and a few little bubbles appear. Whisk into it the sugar, bit by bit , beating well after each addition so you don't add too much by mistake. If you want to use it for piping, don't make it too stiff - experiment with a tiny bit before you're sure.

easy american frosting

I said easy, not quick…. with this method, you don't have to get into sugar thermometers, but it does need a bit of patience and a strong arm. I tend to put a stool – and Radio 4 – within reach of the stove, and try to think of it as free exercise for the pecs (or I cheat and use an electric hand-held mixer).

****

enough to fill and cover an 18-20 cm round or loaf-shaped cake

1 medium egg white
175 g caster sugar
2 tablespoons water
1/2 teaspoon salt
1/2 teaspoon cream of tartar

Put all the ingredients into a heatproof mixing bowl (bigger than you think: the mixture will increase in volume as you beat) over a saucepan of simmering water and whisk everything together with a wire whisk or electric hand-held mixer. Keep beating and it will begin to turn a beautiful, snowy-white. Keep going until it thickens enough to show trails and hold soft peaks as you lift the whisk – by hand it takes me about 9 or 10 minutes, and with a hand-held electric mixer more like 7 or 8. (With an old-fashioned rotary hand beater, to be honest I haven't a clue: I couldn't be bothered to test it a THIRD time…. let's say 8$\frac{1}{2}$). Remove from the heat and spread quickly over the cake.

Vary the flavour by adding a little orange or lemon juice once you start beating and before it thickens. Or add 1 teaspoon of coffee or other type of essence, or use brown sugar instead of the white for a caramel taste.

thermometer american frosting

If you have a cooking thermometer (I definitely recommend one, as you'll have it for years and years and it means you can make jams and other earth-mother kind of things), then this 'proper' way of making American frosting is even easier than the one opposite, and has a slightly better texture. You can also put the thermometer in the oven to check the temperature every now and then.

****

enough to completely cover a 20-23 cm round cake

225 g granulated sugar
60 ml water
pinch of cream of tartar
1 medium egg white

Put the cream of tartar and egg white into a largish bowl and have your hand-held beaters standing by. In a small pan, heat the sugar and water gently, stirring, until the granules are dissolved, then raise the heat and let it boil, without stirring, until it reaches 120°C on the thermometer. (If you find the bulb of the thermometer doesn't quite reach into the liquid, just tip the pan until it does. Check the temperature then put the pan back down on the heat again until the sugar is hot enough). When it's almost there — at about 110°C or so — beat the egg white until stiff and in peaks. As soon as the sugar reaches 120°C, take the pan off the heat. While you let it stand for a few seconds, until most of the bubbles have disappeared, check that the egg white is really stiff, then pour the syrup on to it in a continuous, thin stream, beating all the time. Keep beating the mixture until it is almost cold and thick enough for your recipe (for pouring or peaks).

creamy toffee frosting

****

enough to cover an 20-23 cm round cake, or 18-20 fairy cakes

20 g butter
90 g light brown soft sugar
90 ml sour cream
100 g cream cheese

This is very tasty and easy to spread: it never hardens up and so is a bit sticky to eat, but works well on all kinds of cakes.

Put the butter, sugar and sour cream into a small saucepan and heat carefully, stirring, until the sugar has dissolved. Let it bubble for a few minutes, until it darkens and looks golden brown (the longer you leave it, the stronger the toffee taste will be). Leave it to cool. In a small bowl, beat the cream cheese well until light and fluffy, then gradually add the sugar mixture, beating all the time.

chocolate ganache

****

enough to cover a 20-23 cm round cake

100 g good quality dark chocolate chips

100 ml double cream

1 tablespoon corn or sunflower oil

A rather posh name for a very simple but gorgeous mixture of cream and chocolate. It can be used to pour over cakes and cookies (as for the beautiful Sachertortes you see in smart coffee shops or bakeries) or, if left to cool, it thickens up and is used for piping on to little cakes or even as the base for chocolate truffles. I add a spoonful of corn oil as a way of keeping the icing shiny when it sets – a bit of a cheat, but otherwise you have to get into the relatively complicated business of tempering the chocolate (and you absolutely do not taste the oil, I promise).

Put the chocolate in a heatproof bowl. Heat the cream in a small saucepan until just at boiling point then pour it over the chocolate. Leave it for about 30 seconds, then add the oil and quickly whisk it until all is mixed, smooth and shiny. Leave it to thicken a little until it's the right consistency for coating. If you want to be able to spread or mould the ganache, leave it for longer and in the fridge while it gets firmer.

chocolate frosting

****

enough to fill and cover a 20-23 cm round cake

175 g chocolate chips

450 g icing sugar, sieved

2-3 tablespoons hot water

2 medium egg yolks, lightly beaten

75 g butter, melted

Melt the chocolate in a bowl over hot water, or in the microwave. Stir in the icing sugar with 2 tablespoons of hot water. This will be tricky, and the texture will become very granular, but keep going until it's relatively evenly mixed in, then gradually beat in the egg yolks (I do this part in my electric mixer, or a hand-held one works well) and butter, adding a little more hot water as necessary to reach a smooth, 'spreadable' consistency. Use immediately.

fudgy chocolate icing

****

enough to fill and cover a 20-23 cm
round cake

150 g chocolate chips (dark, milk or
white all work well)
90 g butter
160 ml condensed milk

There's a slightly smoother finish to this one – a bit easier to make than the one above, using condensed milk for the richness rather than the egg yolk. Not so good for swirling, as it tends to stay soft and sticky.

Put everything into a small saucepan and stir over low heat until the chocolate and butter have melted and it becomes a smooth mixture. Remove from the heat and let it cool until it can be spread.

sugarpaste ('roll-out icing') and fondant

I used to make all my own sugarpaste when I first started decorating cakes at home, but, now that there are such good ready-made packets, I honestly don't think it's worth your while. You can buy it in every different colour that you might need, and it'll save so much time and effort for exactly the same result.

sour cream icing

enough for a few fairy cakes or muffins

65 g of sieved icing sugar
15-20 ml sour cream

In a small bowl, gradually beat the sour cream into the icing sugar until smooth.

INDEX